The Old Original

BOOKBINDER'S
RESTAURANT
COOKBOOK

The Old Original

BOOKBINDER'S
RESTAURANT
COOKBOOK

BY CHARLOTTE ADAMS

Thomas Y. Crowell Company

ESTABLISHED 1834

NEW YORK

*With this book the author pays tribute to Vassar College
on the occasion of its centennial.*

Contents

Introduction

When I was asked whether I would be interested in writing the Old Original Bookbinder's cookbook, I jumped at the chance. Like most people in the United States I'd heard of the restaurant all my life. Like a great many who have visited Philadelphia on pleasure or business, I'd eaten many memorable meals there. It has been great fun to put this book together and I've learned a lot in the process.

Samuel Bookbinder established the restaurant in 1865, right after the Civil war. He put it in a most strategic place—near the docks, whence came just-caught fish and seafood and all sorts of choice foods from foreign lands. It was also handy for the sea captains, who became an important part of the clientele. There were many business establishments in the neighborhood, which meant that diners came from insurance firms, banks, import houses—and, not the least important, from the farmers' markets in Dock Street nearby, men who know when food is fresh and good if anyone does.

It is said that in the beginning days Sarah Bookbinder, wife of the founder, used to ring a bell to inform the neighborhood that lunch was ready. That bell still hangs inside the doorway of the restaurant. It sets a tone for the entire decor. Bookbinder's today is a huge place, primarily simple in decor, but with a great and delightful clutter of old playbills, prints, newspaper clippings, and pictures of stage stars. The tables are spacious, whether for two or ten, with comfortable chairs. Almost all the way across the front of the building on the ground floor is a huge clam bar, with built-in steamers for seafood just under the windows and a tank of live lobsters at one end (a source of endless fascination to children who come there—and to their elders, too!). The base of the bar itself and the huge fireplace at the back are made of old cobblestones from Walnut Street, which are worn from the tramping of the Continental and British armies. Lighting fixtures are big ship's wheels. The entrance is an old wheelhouse. There are also ship models, stuffed game fish, and other attractions in abundance.

To the left of the entrance is a big room containing one of the longest and handsomest mahogany bars in existence and a few tables for dining. The walls are hung with pictures of every president of the United States.

There are rooms upstairs, too; some for private parties, one for overflow from the big dining room on ground level. The kitchen is huge, bustling and staffed by some of the nicest men I've met in a long time.

When you come to Philadelphia someone is likely to say to you almost at once: "How about lunch at the Old Original Bookbinder's?" (or dinner, as the case may be). The place is always full of people and it is quite evident that most of them are "regulars." There have always been, and still are, famous guests from the theater and business worlds, ranging from Lillian Russell and Diamond Jim Brady in their day to Danny Kaye and Phil Silvers in our time.

The great specialty of Bookbinder's has always been fish and seafood, and the recipes presented here indicate that trend. The principle of John Taxin, the present owner, is that the reason Bookbinder's food is so good is that he buys only the freshest and best ingredients, which he is inclined to think that housewives do not do. As you would surmise, however, there's more to the success of his restaurant than that. The cooks know their business. For instance, you will find few vegetable recipes here because on the whole only fresh vegetables, cooked to perfection, are served. No one should need recipes for such, though when one eats soggy, overcooked ones elsewhere one thinks that perhaps this is a false assumption! Portions served to guests at Old Original Bookbinder's are enormous, and I have occasionally cut down quantities to what seems to me ample, but not overwhelming, for home use.

You will find that the dishes resulting from these recipes are, by and large, simple, just like those served in the restaurant. The chefs and the owner are inventive about food, but never to the extent of masking the fresh, top-quality ingredients. If you've eaten in the Old Original Bookbinder's you will know that and will be interested in being able to reproduce their dishes. I have taken a few liberties with restaurant recipes in adapting them to home use, but as few as possible, since I am sure that the prime objective of anyone who owns this book will be to prepare meals "just like those at the Old Original Bookbinder's."

Charlotte Adams

Appetizers

CRAB BALLS

    1 tablespoon chopped green pepper
    1 tablespoon minced onion
    1 tablespoon minced celery
    1 tablespoon minced pimiento
      Salt and pepper
    ½ teaspoon thyme
    1 teaspoon Worcestershire sauce
    2 tablespoons butter
    4 tablespoons flour
    1 cup milk
    1 pound crabmeat, well picked over
      Egg Batter (see page 156)
      Bread or cracker crumbs

Mix vegetables and seasonings together and cook in the butter over low heat for 10 minutes, taking care not to brown the vegetables. Add flour and stir to blend well. Cook, stirring, for 5 minutes. Add milk and stir until thickened. Add crabmeat and mix well. Chill the mixture thoroughly. Form into bite-sized balls, dip into egg batter, then into crumbs and fry in deep fat, 375°F., until nicely browned.

Makes 15 to 20 balls.

SHRIMP BITES

> 1 pound large shrimp
> Flour
> Egg Batter (see page 156)
> Corn-flake crumbs
> Lamaze Sauce (see page 148)

Shell and clean shrimp, remove tails, and split in two. Roll in flour. Dip into batter, then roll in crumbs. Fry in deep fat, 375°F., until nicely browned. Serve with Lamaze sauce for dunking.

There should be 16 to 20 shrimp halves.

SHRIMP COCKTAIL

> 6 large, cooked shrimp, thoroughly chilled (see page 74)
> 3 tablespoons cocktail or Lamaze Sauce (see page 148)
> Lemon wedge

Put one tablespoon of sauce in the bottom of each cocktail glass. Place three shrimp on top. Add another tablespoon of sauce, the rest of the shrimp and a third tablespoon of sauce. Serve with a wedge of lemon on the side.

Serves 1.

LOBSTER COCKTAIL

Make exactly as instructed for shrimp cocktail, substituting ½ cup cooked lobster meat for the shrimp.

CRABMEAT COCKTAIL

Make exactly as instructed for shrimp cocktail, substituting ½ cup cooked crabmeat for the shrimp.

CLAMS (OR OYSTERS) CASINO

    6 cherrystone clams on the halfshell
    2 tablespoons finely chopped green pepper
    2 tablespoons finely chopped pimiento
    1 strip bacon, cut in small pieces
    1 tablespoon melted butter
      Paprika

Place clams in a tin plate, half filled with rock salt (use enough rock salt to hold the shellfish firmly in place). Sprinkle each with bits of green pepper and pimiento. Place pieces of bacon on top. Sprinkle with melted butter and a dash of paprika. Bake in a hot oven, 400°F., for 10 minutes. Turn bacon once so that it will crisp on both sides.
    Serves 1.

Note: Oysters Casino also appear on Bookbinder's menu as "Barbecued Oysters."

OYSTERS ROCKEFELLER

    6 oysters on the halfshell
      Rock salt
    1 teaspoon butter
    1 teaspoon finely minced onion

1 teaspoon finely minced celery
Flour
2 tablespoons chopped, cooked spinach
Salt and pepper
Nutmeg
¼ teaspoon Worcestershire sauce
1 tablespoon Parmesan cheese
1 tablespoon bread crumbs
Butter

Melt the teaspoon of butter. Sauté onion and celery in it until soft, but not brown. Dredge lightly with flour. Season spinach to taste with salt and pepper. Give it a good grind of fresh nutmeg and add Worcestershire sauce. Place oysters on a bed of rock salt (enough to hold them firmly in place) in a pie plate. Place in a moderate oven, 375°F., to heat for 3 to 4 minutes. Mix onion and celery with spinach mixture. Remove oysters from the oven and cover each with spinach mixture. Mix the cheese and bread crumbs and sprinkle over the oysters. Dot each lightly with butter. Return oysters to the oven and bake 10 to 12 minutes, or until brown.

Serves 1.

HERRING IN SOUR CREAM

8 herring in brine
2 cups white vinegar
3 cups water
1 brimming cup sugar
1 large sweet Bermuda onion
2 cups sour cream
1 cup buttermilk

Fillet the herring. Soak at least 24 hours in fresh water to remove brine. Drain. Mix vinegar, water, and sugar thoroughly so that sugar is entirely dissolved. Pour the vinegar mixture over the herring. Place in refrigerator for three days, turning twice a day. When ready to serve, drain herring thoroughly. Slice onion thinly into rings and place rings on top of fillets. Cover with sour cream and buttermilk, well mixed.

Serves 4 to 8, depending upon appetites.

Note: The more usual way to do this for home use is to cover the marinated herring with onion slices and sour cream and let it stand, covered, in the refrigerator overnight.

BROILED MEAT STICKS

   1 pound ground chuck
 ½ cup bread crumbs
   1 egg, beaten
     Salt and pepper
     Dash of cayenne
   1 teaspoon Worcestershire sauce

Mix all ingredients. Form into sticks, about three inches long. Broil, turning to brown all sides.

Makes 15 to 20 sticks.

Soups

FISH CHOWDER

¼ pound salt pork, cubed
1 cup chopped onion
3 cups diced uncooked potatoes
1 teaspoon salt
3 pounds fresh haddock, skinned but not boned
1 cup heavy cream
2 tablespoons butter
Freshly ground pepper to taste

Try out the pork cubes. When they are crisp, remove the cracklings. Fry the onion in the pork fat until lightly brown. Add potatoes and half the salt. Cover with water and cook 15 to 20 minutes, until potatoes are tender, but not broken. Drain. Cut the fish into three pieces and simmer in boiling water with the remaining salt until it flakes easily with a fork (15 to 20 minutes). Strain, reserving stock. Remove bones from fish and break it into large pieces. Return to stock, adding potato and onion mixture. Add cream, butter, and pepper. Simmer until heated through. Sprinkle the cracklings over the chowder just before serving.

Serves 4 to 5.

BOUILLABAISSE SOUP

½ pound shrimp
½ pound codfish
½ pound scallops
6 oysters
2 tablespoons minced onion
1 clove garlic, mashed
2 tablespoons minced celery
2 tablespoons minced green pepper
½ cup butter
½ cup flour
2 cups stock from fish
1 cup cooked lobster meat

Shell and clean the shrimp, saving the shells. Tie the codfish in cheesecloth. Place the codfish, scallops, shrimp, and oysters in salted water to cover. Bring to boiling, then reduce heat and simmer 5 minutes. Drain, reserving stock. Place shrimp shells in stock and cook it until it is reduced to 4 cups. Strain through a cheesecloth. Meantime, cook onion, garlic, celery, and green pepper in butter until soft, but not brown. Add flour and stir thoroughly until smooth. Add 2 cups stock and stir until thickened. Dice the codfish, lobster, scallops, and shrimp. Add to thickened soup and heat through. You will have 2 cups fish stock left for future use; store it in a covered jar in the refrigerator.

Serves 6.

BOOKBINDER'S CLAM CHOWDER

     1 cup large chowder clams
     3 ounces salt pork, diced
     1 medium onion, sliced
     1 large potato, diced
     1 tablespoon flour
        Salt and pepper
     1 cup boiling water
     2 cups milk, scalded
     1 tablespoon butter

Drain clams, reserving liquor. Fry pork to golden brown, then add onion and fry to light golden. Add a layer of potatoes and sprinkle with flour, salt, and pepper. Add clams, then another layer of potatoes, sprinkled with the remainder of the flour and with salt and pepper. Add boiling water and simmer until potatoes are done (18 to 20 minutes). Combine milk, clam liquor, and butter; add to the clam mixture. Simmer 5 minutes. Serve with crackers.

Makes 2 generous servings or 4 small ones.

Note: To make a richer chowder, substitute light cream for the milk.

CRAB STEW

     ½ cup butter
     2 teaspoons powdered chicken stock
     2 tablespoons flour
     6 cups milk

Salt
Dash white pepper
2 cups crabmeat

Melt butter. Add powdered chicken stock and flour and mix until smooth. Add milk gradually and stir constantly until it comes *just* to the boil. Season to taste with salt and pepper, add crabmeat, and heat through.

Serves 4.

LOBSTER STEW

2 1-pound Maine lobsters
½ cup butter
1 quart light cream (or half milk, half cream)

Boil lobsters and remove meat immediately. Also save the tomalley or liver, the coral and the fat. Simmer the tomalley and coral in butter in a heavy kettle for 7 or 8 minutes. Cut the lobster into fairly large pieces; add it and the fat to the tomalley and coral. Cook all together 3 minutes over low heat. Remove from heat. Allow to cool slightly and then slowly add cream, stirring constantly. Return to heat and heat through but do not boil.

Serves 4.

LOBSTER BISQUE

    1 tablespoon finely minced celery
    1 tablespoon finely minced onion
    3 tablespoons butter
¼ cup flour
    4 cups lobster stock
¼ cup cream
      Salt and white pepper
      Dash of freshly ground nutmeg
    1 cup diced lobster meat

Sauté celery and onion in butter until soft, but not brown. Sprinkle with the flour and mix well. Add lobster stock and cream and stir until thickened. Season to taste with salt, white pepper, and nutmeg. Add lobster meat and heat through.

    Serves 4.

OYSTER STEW

1½ dozen oysters
  2 cups milk
  2 cups light cream
  2 tablespoons butter
    Salt and pepper
    Paprika

Cook oysters in their own liquid over low heat until the edges curl. Scald milk and cream and add to oysters. Add butter and season to taste with salt, pepper, and paprika.

    Serves 3.

SCALLOP STEW

2 cups (1 pint) milk
2 cups (1 pint) light cream
⅓ cup butter
½ teaspoon Worcestershire sauce
1 pound scallops
   Salt and pepper

Heat milk and cream in a double boiler. Melt butter and add Worcestershire. Dice scallops coarsely (unless you use little bay scallops, then leave them whole). Add to butter and Worcestershire. Simmer until tender (about 5 minutes). Add to milk and cream. Add salt and pepper to taste. Allow to stand in double boiler over low heat 5 to 10 minutes to meld the flavors.

Serves 4 to 6.

SHRIMP CHOWDER

¼ cup chopped onions
6 tablespoons butter
2 tablespoons flour
   Salt
   Cayenne pepper
   Blade of mace
4 cups hot milk
2 cups cooked shrimp
1 cup hot cream

Sauté the chopped onions in 4 tablespoons (½ stick) butter until soft and golden. In a separate saucepan melt 2 tablespoons butter.

Combine flour and seasonings and add to melted butter, stirring to blend well. Add milk gradually; stir constantly until smooth and thickened. Place over hot, not boiling, water, and add shrimp. Continue cooking for 20 minutes. Remove blade of mace. Strain onion butter and add to shrimp along with hot cream. Heat but do not boil.

Serves 4.

CREAM OF SHRIMP SOUP

1 pound shrimp
1 tablespoon minced onion
1 tablespoon minced celery
2 tablespoons butter or oil
2 tablespoons flour
1 cup shrimp liquor
1 cup cream

Place shrimp in boiling, salted water to barely cover them, and cook 10 to 15 minutes, depending on the size of the shrimp. Drain, reserving liquor. Peel, return shells to the shrimp liquor, and clean and chop the shrimp. Boil the shells in the liquor until it is reduced in quantity to about 1 cup. Strain through a cheese-cloth. Cook onion and celery in butter or oil over low heat until soft, but not brown. Add flour and stir to mix in smoothly. Add shrimp liquor and cream and stir until thickened. Add chopped shrimp and heat through.

Serves 4.

SNAPPER SOUP

3½ pounds veal knuckle
1 cup chicken fat or butter
3 onions, chopped fine
2 stalks celery, chopped
2 carrots, diced
½ teaspoon thyme
½ teaspoon marjoram
3 whole cloves
1 bay leaf
   Salt and pepper
1 cup flour
4 quarts beef broth
2 cups strained tomatoes
   Meat from 1 snapper turtle, cut in small pieces
2 cups dry sherry
   Dash of Tabasco
3 slices lemon
1 hard-cooked egg, chopped

Have knuckles broken into 2-inch pieces. Place knuckles in a roasting pan and add the butter or chicken fat, onions, celery, carrots, thyme, marjoram, cloves, bay leaf, salt, and pepper. Bake in a hot (400°F.) oven until brown (about 30 minutes). Remove from oven and add flour, mixing well. Reduce oven heat to 350°F. and cook 30 minutes longer. Pour mixture into a large soup kettle. Add broth and tomatoes. Cook at a simmer for 3½ hours. Combine the snapper meat with 1 cup dry sherry, a dash of salt and Tabasco, and the lemon slices. Simmer for 10 minutes. Strain the soup and combine with the snapper mixture. Add chopped egg and the remaining 1 cup dry sherry. Heat through and serve at once.

This makes a little over a gallon.

Note: If you cannot get snapper turtle to make this soup yourself, you may order the soup in cans from Bookbinder's.

CHICKEN GUMBO SOUP

½ package frozen okra
6 cups chicken stock
¼ cup chopped celery
¼ cup chopped onions
1 cup stewed tomatoes
½ cup cooked rice
Salt and pepper

Run hot water over the okra to defrost it. Slice it and add to the chicken stock with celery, onions, tomatoes, and rice. Simmer for half an hour. Season to taste with salt and pepper.

Serves 4.

CHICKEN NOODLE SOUP

1 5-pound stewing chicken
2 stalks celery
1 medium onion, peeled
½ cup finely minced celery
½ cup finely minced onion
½ pound fine noodles

Put chicken, celery stalks, and onion into a kettle and cover completely with salted water. Bring to boiling, then lower the heat and simmer until chicken is tender (about 2 hours). Remove chicken. Skin the chicken and take meat from bones. Return skin and bones to stock and simmer until it is reduced to about half. Cook minced celery and onion in a bit of the stock until very tender (about 10 minutes). Strain stock, add cooked celery and onion and the noodles and boil 9 minutes.

Serves 4 to 6.

Note: ½ cup uncooked rice may be substituted for the noodles, in which case it should be boiled for 14 minutes.

CHICKEN VEGETABLE SOUP

1 quart chicken stock
1 tablespoon powdered chicken stock
¼ cup diced green beans
¼ cup shelled peas
¼ cup diced carrots
¼ cup diced celery
¼ cup diced onion
   Salt and pepper

Simmer vegetables in the chicken stock, enriched with the powdered stock, until done (15 to 20 minutes). Season to taste with salt and pepper.

Serves 4.

BEEF CONSOMME

>   3 quarts beef stock
>   3 pounds beef bones with meat
>   2 carrots, cut up
>   2 onions, cut coarsely
>   2 stalks celery, cut up
>   1 clove garlic
>   Salt and pepper
>   Powdered beef stock, if desired

Simmer beef bones and vegetables in stock until meat falls off bones (2 to 3 hours). Strain. Correct seasoning and add powdered beef stock if a stronger flavor is desired. Bookbinder's serves this with strips of cooked beef and noodles or rice in it. It may also be served clear.

Serves 6 to 8.

BEEF BARLEY SOUP

>   6 cups beef consommé
>   3 tablespoons barley
>   ¼ cup chopped celery
>   ¼ cup chopped onions
>   1 tablespoon powdered beef stock

Combine all ingredients and cook over medium heat for half an hour. Correct seasoning and serve.

Serves 4.

OXTAIL SOUP

> 1 oxtail
> Salt and pepper
> Flour
> 2 tablespoons fat
> 2 stalks celery
> 1 medium onion, peeled
> 1 bay leaf
> Beef stock to cover
> ⅓ cup diced celery
> ⅓ cup diced onion
> ⅓ cup diced carrots
> 1 clove garlic, mashed
> Sherry to taste, if desired

Have the oxtail cut into small pieces. Season with salt and pepper. Dredge with flour and brown in fat. Add celery stalks, whole peeled onion, bay leaf, and beef stock. Simmer 2 to 3 hours, or until meat is tender. Strain, reserving stock. Remove meat from bones and return meat to stock with the diced vegetables and garlic. Cook until vegetables are tender (about 20 minutes). Correct seasoning and add sherry to taste, if desired.

Serves 4 to 6.

VEGETABLE BEEF SOUP

    1 pound chuck, cut in Julienne strips
    2 quarts beef stock
    ¼ cup diced green beans
    ¼ cup shelled peas
    ¼ cup diced carrots
    ¼ cup diced celery
    1 tablespoon minced onion
      Salt and pepper

Cook the strips of beef in the beef stock until tender (about 45 minutes). Add vegetables and cook until tender (about 15 minutes). Season to taste with salt and pepper and serve.

    Serves 6.

VEGETABLE SOUP

    2 quarts veal or chicken stock
    ½ cup shelled peas
    ½ cup cut-up green beans,
    ½ cup diced carrots
    2 tablespoons diced onion
    ½ cup diced celery
    ½ cup diced tomatoes
    ½ cup diced potatoes
      Salt and pepper

Place stock and vegetables in kettle. Season to taste with salt and pepper. Bring to boiling, reduce heat, and simmer, covered, about

½ hour or until vegetables are done to your taste. Correct seasoning and serve.

Serves 6.

CREAMED VEGETABLE SOUP

6 cups ham stock (or salted water)
½ cup shelled peas
½ cup cut green beans
3 carrots, diced
3 stalks celery, diced
¼ cup butter
¼ cup flour
¼ cup cream
   Salt and pepper

Cook vegetables in ham stock or salted water until done (about 20 minutes). Drain, reserving stock. Melt butter. Stir in flour smoothly. Add cream and vegetable stock and stir constantly until thickened. Add vegetables and heat through. Season to taste with salt and pepper.

Serves 6.

PEPPER POT SOUP

  1 pound honeycomb tripe
  6 cups beef stock
  1 medium green pepper, diced
  ¼ cup diced celery
  ¼ cup diced onion
  1 cup stewed tomatoes
  1 cup diced uncooked potatoes
     or 1 cup shell macaroni
  ¼ teaspoon thyme
  1 small clove garlic, mashed
     Dash of Tabasco
     Salt and pepper
  ¼ cup bacon fat
  ¼ cup flour

Cook the tripe in one piece in the stock about 3 hours, or until tender. Drain, reserving stock. Cool, chill, and cut into strips. If there are not 4 cups of tripe stock, add enough beef stock to make it up to 4 cups. Add green pepper, celery, onion, tomatoes, and potatoes or macaroni, together with the seasonings, and cook until vegetables are done (about 20 minutes). Melt bacon fat and add flour, stirring until smooth. Add stock and vegetables and stir until thickened. Add tripe and heat through. Correct seasoning.

Serves 4 to 6.

CREAM OF ASPARAGUS SOUP

  1 bunch asparagus
  6 cups chicken stock

¼ cup minced celery
¼ cup minced onion
   Salt and pepper
¼ cup butter
¼ cup flour
½ cup cream

Cut off woody, thick ends of asparagus. Tie tips together in a bunch and cook until just tender in the chicken stock with celery and onion. Remove asparagus and cut into ½-inch pieces. Season stock to taste with salt and pepper. Melt butter and blend in flour smoothly. Add cream and asparagus stock and stir until thickened. Add diced asparagus and heat through.

Serves 6.

CORN CHOWDER

¼ pound fat salt pork, diced
1 tablespoon minced onion
1 tablespoon minced green pepper
1 tablespoon minced celery
2 cups fresh, uncooked corn kernels
1 cup cooked, diced potato
6 cups rich milk, scalded
   Salt and pepper

Try out the pork dice until crisp and brown. Remove browned dice and cook the onion, green pepper and celery in the fat 5 minutes over low heat, stirring frequently. Add corn and milk and cook at a simmer for 5 minutes. Add potato and let heat through. Season to taste with salt and pepper. Serve with crisp pork bits scattered on top.

Serves 4 to 6.

LENTIL SOUP

    1 cup lentils
       Ham bone
   ½ cup coarsely chopped onions
   ½ cup chopped celery
       Salt and pepper
       Bay leaf
       Sliced frankfurters

Soak lentils overnight in water to cover. Drain. Add ham bone and water to cover and simmer, covered, for three hours. Add onions and celery. Season to taste with salt and pepper. Add bay leaf and simmer, covered, for another hour. Remove ham bone and bay leaf and serve with sliced frankfurters, well heated, floating on top.

    Serves 6.

PUREE MONGOLE

    1 cup split peas
       Ham bone
   ½ cup chopped onions
   ½ cup chopped celery
   ½ cup diced carrots
   ½ cup diced green beans
 1½ cups canned tomatoes
       Salt and pepper

Soak peas overnight in water to cover. Drain. Add ham bone and fresh water to cover and simmer, covered, for three hours. Add remaining ingredients and continue cooking, covered, for an hour. Remove ham bone and press remaining mixture through a sieve or whirl in the blender. If the soup is too thick for your taste you may add milk or cream to thin it. If it is not thick enough, add a roux of butter and flour. Season to taste.

Serves 6.

SPLIT PEA SOUP WITH BUTTER CROUTONS

    1 cup split peas
    Ham or veal bone
  ½ cup coarsely chopped onions
  ½ cup chopped celery
    Salt and pepper
    Dash of thyme

Soak peas overnight in water to cover. Drain. Add ham or veal bone and water to cover (ham stock is even better, if you've just boiled a ham) and simmer, covered, for three hours. Add celery and onions. Season to taste with salt, pepper, and thyme. Cook, covered, for another hour. Remove bone. Correct seasoning and press through a sieve or whirl in the blender.

Serves 6.

BUTTER CROUTONS

    1 cup bread cubes
    2 tablespoons butter

Sauté the bread cubes in butter (adding more, if necessary), turning them constantly to brown on all sides, and taking care not to burn them. Sprinkle over soup just at serving time.

YANKEE BEAN SOUP

 1 cup navy beans
  Ham bone
  Ham stock or water
 ½ cup coarsely chopped onions
 ½ cup chopped celery
  Salt and pepper
  Bay leaf

Soak beans overnight in water to cover. Drain. Add ham bone and ham stock or water to cover and simmer, covered, for 3 hours. Add chopped celery and onions, season to taste with salt and pepper, and add the bay leaf. Cook, covered, for another hour. Remove bone and bay leaf. Correct seasoning and serve.
 Serves 6.

TOMATO BISQUE

 2 pounds ripe tomatoes, diced
 2 medium onions, diced
 ½ cup diced celery
 1 carrot, diced
  Carcass of fowl
  Chicken stock to cover (4 to 6 cups)
  Salt and pepper
  Dash of fresh-ground nutmeg
 ¼ cup butter ⎫
 ¼ cup flour ⎬ for thickening, if desired
 2 cups cream

Place vegetables, carcass of fowl, and stock in kettle. Bring to the boil and simmer, covered, 1 hour. Remove fowl carcass and whirl soup in the blender or press through a sieve. Season to taste with salt, pepper, and nutmeg. Thicken, if desired, with butter and flour smoothly blended. Add cream and heat through.

Serves 6 to 8.

Note: This soup, unthickened, is sometimes served at Bookbinder's with cooked rice in it or with mixed cooked vegetables.

Eggs
and
Cheese

PLAIN OMELET

> 2 eggs
> Salt and pepper
> 1 tablespoon butter

Beat eggs with a fork until yolks and whites are well mixed. Season with salt and freshly ground pepper. Melt the butter in an omelet pan over fairly high heat. When it sizzles, pour in the eggs and stir them once, quickly. Cook only until set on under side (1 to 2 minutes). Fold omelet in from both sides and roll it out of the pan onto hot serving plate. Serve at once.
Serves 1.

JELLY OMELET

> 2 eggs
> Salt and pepper
> 1 tablespoon butter
> 3 tablespoons currant jelly

Beat the eggs with a fork to mix thoroughly. Season with salt and pepper. Melt butter in an omelet pan over fairly high heat until sizzling. Pour in eggs and stir once, quickly. Put jelly over

34

the surface of the omelet. Fold and roll the omelet onto a hot plate. Serve at once.

Serves 1.

Note: Other jellies and jams can be used to suit your taste.

CHEESE OMELET

    3 eggs
    2 tablespoons grated sharp cheese
      Salt and pepper
    1 tablespoon butter

Beat eggs with a fork to mix thoroughly. Beat in 1 tablespoon of the grated sharp cheese. Season with salt and pepper. Melt the butter in an omelet pan over fairly high heat. When the butter is sizzling, pour in the eggs and give them one quick stir. Sprinkle the remaining tablespoon of cheese over the eggs. Fold the omelet and roll it onto a hot plate. Serve at once.

Serves 2.

Note: The above mixture can be used as filling for two sandwiches. In this case do not fold, but turn the omelet to brown lightly on both sides.

MUSHROOM OMELET

    2 large mushrooms, diced
    2 tablespoons butter
      Salt and pepper
    2 eggs

Sauté diced mushrooms in 1 tablespoon butter for about 5 minutes. Season to taste with salt and pepper. Beat eggs with a fork until well mixed. Season with salt and pepper. Melt another tablespoon of butter in an omelet pan over fairly high heat; when it is sizzling, pour in eggs and stir them once, quickly. Sprinkle sautéed mushrooms over the eggs. Fold the omelet and roll it onto a hot plate. Serve at once.

Serves 1.

TOMATO OMELET

½ cup stewed tomatoes with juice
½ teaspoon sugar
Salt and pepper
¼ teaspoon dried basil
1 teaspoon chopped onion
2 teaspoons cornstarch
2 eggs
Salt and pepper
1 tablespoon butter

Heat tomatoes with sugar, salt, pepper, basil, and onion. Mix a little of the juice with the cornstarch to blend well. Return to tomato mixture and stir to blend and thicken. Beat eggs with a fork to blend thoroughly. Season with salt and pepper. Melt butter in an omelet pan over fairly high heat. When the butter is sizzling, pour in the eggs. Stir once, quickly, and pour half the tomato mixture over the eggs. Fold the omelet and roll it onto a hot plate. Pour rest of tomato mixture over the omelet. Serve at once.

Serves 1.

SPANISH OMELET

    1 cup Creole Sauce (see page 146)
    3 eggs
      Salt and pepper
    1 tablespoon butter

Heat Creole Sauce. Beat eggs with a fork to blend thoroughly. Season with salt and pepper. Melt butter over fairly high heat, and when it is sizzling pour in eggs. Pour half the Creole Sauce over the eggs, fold the omelet, and roll it onto a hot plate. Pour the rest of the sauce over all. Serve at once.
    Serves 2.

ONION OMELET

    1 medium onion, thinly sliced
    1 tablespoon butter
    2 eggs
      Salt and pepper

Sauté onion in butter until soft, but not brown (about 10 minutes). Beat eggs with a fork to mix thoroughly. Season with salt and pepper. Turn up heat to fairly high. Pour eggs over the onions and stir once, quickly. Cook only until set on under side (1 to 2 minutes). Fold the omelet and roll it onto a hot serving plate. Serve at once.
    Serves 1.

SHAD ROE OMELET

1 small shad roe
1 teaspoon minced onion
1 tablespoon butter
6 eggs
    Salt and pepper

Steam the shad roe in a very little water until cooked but not dry. Sauté the onion in butter until soft, but not brown. Chop up the roe lightly. Add to onion. Beat eggs with a fork. Season with salt and pepper. Pour over shad roe and cook just until set. Fold the omelet and roll it onto a hot plate.
    Serves 3.

LOBSTER OMELET

2 eggs
    Salt and pepper
1 tablespoon butter
¼ cup diced, cooked lobster
¼ cup Newburg Sauce (see page 150)

Heat the lobster in the Newburg Sauce. Make omelet according to directions for Plain Omelet (see page 34). When folded and placed on serving plate, pour over it the lobster and Newburg Sauce. Serve at once.
    Serves 1.

SHRIMP OMELET

Make exactly as Lobster Omelet, substituting diced, cooked shrimp for the lobster.

OYSTER OMELET

> 6 oysters
> 2 tablespoons butter
> 1 tablespoon flour
> ½ cup oyster liquor and cream
>   Salt and pepper
> 3 eggs
>   Parsley

Drain oysters, reserving liquor. Melt 1 tablespoon butter and simmer oysters in it until the edges curl. Sprinkle flour over the oysters and blend thoroughly. Measure oyster liquor and add cream to make ½ cup. Add to oysters and stir constantly until thickened. Season to taste with salt and pepper. Beat eggs with a fork to mix thoroughly. Season with salt and pepper. Melt another tablespoon of butter over fairly high heat, and when it is sizzling pour in eggs. Stir them once, quickly. Pour oysters over the eggs immediately, reserving a little of the sauce. Fold omelet and roll it onto a hot plate. Pour remaining sauce over one end of the omelet. Decorate with sprigs of parsley. Serve at once.
   Serves 2.

CHICKEN LIVER OMELET

     2 chicken livers
     2 tablespoons butter
       Salt and pepper
     2 eggs

Chop the chicken livers coarsely and sauté in 1 tablespoon butter until done to your taste (5 to 8 minutes). Season with salt and pepper. Beat the eggs with a fork to mix thoroughly. Season with salt and pepper. Melt another tablespoon of butter over fairly high heat, and when it is sizzling, pour in the eggs. Give one quick stir and then pour cooked chicken livers over the eggs. Fold the omelet and roll it onto a hot plate.
     Serves 1.

HAM OMELET

     3 eggs
       Salt and pepper
     ½ cup finely diced cooked ham
     1 tablespoon butter

Beat the eggs with a fork to mix thoroughly. Season with salt and pepper. Add ham and mix. Melt butter in an omelet pan over fairly high heat. When the butter is sizzling, pour in the egg mixture. Stir once, quickly, and cook until omelet is set on the bottom (1 to 2 minutes). Fold the omelet and roll it onto a hot plate. Serve at once.
     Serves 2.

Note: This can also be made into two sandwiches. In that case, brown the omelet on both sides and, of course, do not fold.

WESTERN OMELET

> 1 small onion, diced
> 2 tablespoons diced green pepper
> 3 tablespoons diced ham
>   *or* 3 tablespoons diced, partially cooked bacon
> 1 tablespoon butter
> 3 eggs
>   Salt and pepper

Sauté onion, green pepper, and ham or bacon in the butter over low heat for 10 minutes, or until the onions and peppers are soft but not brown. Beat eggs with a fork until well mixed; add salt and pepper. Turn up heat to fairly high. Pour eggs over the vegetables and ham and stir once, quickly. Cook only until set on under side (1 to 2 minutes). Fold the omelet and roll it onto a hot serving plate. Serve at once.

Serves 2.

Note: Left flat (not folded), this makes the filling for two Western Egg Sandwiches.

SALAMI OMELET

> ½ cup coarsely chopped salami
> 2 tablespoons butter
> 2 eggs
>   Salt and pepper

Cook salami in the butter for 5 minutes over low heat, stirring frequently. Beat eggs with a fork; season with salt and pepper. Pour over salami and allow to set on the bottom. Fold the omelet, roll it onto a hot plate, and serve at once.

Serves 1.

SALAMI AND EGGS

2 ¼-inch-thick slices salami
1 tablespoon butter
2 eggs
Salt and pepper

Simmer the salami slices in butter at low heat, to warm, but not brown. Break an egg over each slice. Season with salt and pepper. Place under the broiler until the eggs are done to your taste.

Serves 1.

SALAMI AND EGGS, PANCAKE STYLE

2 ¼-inch-thick slices salami
1 tablespoon butter
2 eggs
Salt and pepper

Heat salami slices in butter. Beat the eggs with a fork and season with salt and pepper. Pour the eggs over salami slices and allow to brown to golden on the under side. Turn and brown second side, if desired.

Serves 1.

WELSH RAREBIT

1 cup grated sharp cheese
½ cup cream
1 tablespoon butter
½ teaspoon salt
¼ teaspoon dry mustard
  Dash of Worcestershire sauce

Over boiling water, melt the grated sharp cheese in the cream and butter, stirring constantly with a wooden spoon until well blended. Add seasonings and serve on toast.
  Serves 2.

WELSH RAREBIT WITH BEER

1 cup grated sharp cheese
½ cup stale beer
1 tablespoon butter
½ teaspoon salt
½ teaspoon dry mustard
  Dash of Worcestershire sauce

Over boiling water, melt the grated sharp cheese in the beer and butter, stirring constantly with a wooden spoon until well blended. Add seasonings and serve on toast.
  Serves 2.

Note: Rarebit can be served as an open sandwich. Place tomato slices and a slice of crisp bacon on a piece of toast. Pour rarebit over all.

CHEESE-TOMATO RAREBIT

>2 tablespoons butter
>2 tablespoons flour
>1 cup cream
>½ cup canned tomatoes, well drained and mashed
>2 cups grated sharp cheese
>¼ teaspoon dry mustard
>½ teaspoon salt
>Dash of cayenne pepper

Over boiling water, melt the butter. Add flour and stir until smooth. Add cream and stir until thickened. Add tomatoes, well mashed, and the grated sharp cheese. Stir until well blended. Add seasonings and serve on toast.

Serves 2.

SHRIMP RAREBIT

>1 cup grated sharp cheese
>½ cup cream
>1 tablespoon butter
>½ teaspoon salt
>¼ teaspoon dry mustard
>Dash of Worcestershire sauce
>½ cup diced, cooked shrimp

Over boiling water, melt grated sharp cheese in the cream and butter, stirring constantly with a wooden spoon until well blended. Add seasonings and shrimp and heat through, stirring constantly. Serve on toasted English muffins.

Serves 2.

Seafood

SEAFOOD O'BRIEN

    1 cup cooked lobster
    1 cup steamed scallops
    1 cup cooked shrimp
    ½ cup green pepper strips
    ½ cup pimiento strips
    3 tablespoons butter
      Salt and pepper
    ½ cup red wine

Sauté seafood, pepper strips, and pimiento strips in butter for about 5 minutes over moderate heat. Do not brown. Season with salt and pepper to taste. Put into casserole and add wine. Heat through, but do not overcook.

    Serves 6.

CLAMBURGERS

    1 pint clams, chopped fine
    1 egg, well beaten
    1 cup cracker crumbs
    1 teaspoon salt
    ¼ teaspoon pepper

Combine all ingredients and mix well. Form into round patties and fry in 1-inch-deep hot fat until nicely browned (8 to 10 minutes). Drain on absorbent paper. Serve piping hot.

Serves 4.

DEVILED CLAMS

1 tablespoon chopped onion
1 tablespoon chopped green pepper
1 tablespoon chopped celery
2 tablespoons butter
6 tablespoons flour
2 teaspoons dry mustard
   Tabasco sauce to taste
½ teaspoon thyme
2 cans chopped clams, drained, reserving liquor
2 cups clam liquor and milk
   Salt and white pepper
   Corn-flake crumbs

Fry onions, green pepper, and celery in butter until soft but not brown. Add flour and dry mustard, and mix thoroughly into a stiff roux. Add Tabasco and thyme; mix well. Add clam liquor mixed with enough milk to make 2 cups. Stir constantly until well blended and thick. Stir in clams, then add salt and white pepper to taste. Place the mixture in big clam shells (or use the scallop shells you can buy in houseware departments). Sprinkle with crumbs and dot lightly with extra butter. Bake in a moderate (375°F.) oven 20 minutes, or until nicely browned.

Serves 6.

Restaurant Method: After filling the shells, dip into flour, then Egg Batter (see page 156), then corn-flake crumbs. Fry in deep fat (375°F.) for 6 to 8 minutes or until nicely browned. With this method you get a crisper crust, but for most housewives the baking procedure is simpler.

FRIED CLAMS

   1 egg, separated
½ cup milk
   1 tablespoon melted butter
¼ teaspoon salt
½ cup flour, sifted
24 cherrystone or Ipswich clams, cleaned and drained

Beat egg yolk until thick and lemon-colored. Add milk and butter and blend thoroughly. Sift flour and salt together, add to egg mixture, and stir until smooth. Beat egg white until stiff and fold into egg yolk mixture. Dip each clam into the batter and fry in deep hot (375°F.) fat until golden brown. Turn frequently to brown all sides. Drain on absorbent paper.

Serves 4.

FRIED CLAM FRITTERS

   1 pint fresh clams, ground
   2 cups flour
   1 teaspoon baking powder
½ teaspoon salt
   2 eggs, well beaten
½ cup milk

½ cup clam liquor
Deep fat for frying

Sift together flour, baking powder, and salt. Slowly add eggs, milk, and clam liquor. Blend thoroughly. Add ground clams. Drop by large tablespoonsful into deep hot (375°F.) fat. Fry until nicely browned. Remove and drain on absorbent paper.
Serves 4.

STEAMED CLAMS

Scrub the shells and carefully wash free of sand in several waters. Place in a large kettle with two cups of water. Cover and steam until shells open. Serve the clams while still very hot, with side dishes of melted butter and clam broth.
Allow 15 to 20 clams for each serving.

CRABMEAT AU GRATIN

1 pound lump crabmeat
4 tablespoons butter
4 tablespoons flour
2 cups light cream
Salt and pepper
½ cup dry bread crumbs
½ cup grated cheese
Butter for dotting

Melt 4 tablespoons butter and blend in flour, stirring until smooth. Add cream and cook over medium heat, stirring constantly, until thickened. Add crabmeat and continue cooking just long enough for the crabmeat to heat through. Season to taste with salt and pepper. Put into shallow, individual ovenproof dishes. Mix bread crumbs and cheese and sprinkle over the tops. Dot with butter. Place under broiler and heat until golden brown.

Serves 4.

SPECIAL BAKED CRAB

2 pounds crabmeat
¼ cup butter
¼ cup flour
2 cups milk or light cream
Salt and pepper
¼ cup mayonnaise
6 tablespoons minced parsley
2 egg yolks, well beaten
Paprika

Melt butter. Add flour and stir until smooth. Add milk and cook over medium heat, stirring constantly, until thickened. Season to taste with salt and pepper. Add mayonnaise, parsley, egg yolks, and crabmeat and mix well. Pile into individual casseroles or shells, and sprinkle with paprika. Bake in a moderate (375°F.) oven 12 to 15 minutes.

Serves 6.

Note: At Bookbinder's the chefs use a very heavy cream sauce, almost like a paste. I think that for home use you will like this one better.

CRAB CAKES MARYLAND STYLE

¼ cup (½ stick) butter
½ cup flour
2 cups milk
1 egg, beaten
1 teaspoon salt
¼ teaspoon dry mustard
1 tablespoon Worcestershire sauce
2 tablespoons chopped fresh parsley
2 pounds lump crabmeat
  Egg Batter (see page 156)
  Bread or cracker crumbs

Melt butter and blend in flour, stirring until smooth. Add milk and stir until thickened. Beat in the egg. Add salt, dry mustard, Worcestershire sauce, and parsley; mix well. Cool. Stir in crabmeat. Form into large cakes and chill thoroughly. Dip cakes in Egg Batter, then in crumbs, and fry in deep hot fat (375°F.) until nicely browned (about 15 minutes).

Serves 6.

DEVILED CRAB

½ cup diced green pepper
½ cup diced onion
¼ cup diced celery
1 pimiento, diced
1 teaspoon salt
½ teaspoon black pepper
1 teaspoon thyme
1 tablespoon Worcestershire sauce
Dash Tabasco sauce
1 teaspoon dry mustard
¼ cup (½ stick) butter
½ cup flour
2 cups milk
2 pounds crabmeat, well picked over
Bread crumbs
Butter

Melt ½ stick butter. Add green pepper, onion, celery, pimiento, and seasonings and cook in the butter over low heat for 10 minutes. Add flour and stir until smooth. Cook another 5 minutes, stirring constantly. Add milk and stir until the sauce becomes very thick. Stir in the crabmeat. Mound into shells or individual casseroles. Cover with bread crumbs and dot with butter. Bake in a hot (400°F.) oven until nicely browned (about 20 minutes).
    Serves 6.

Note: This same mixture can be chilled; formed into cakes, dipped in flour, Egg Batter (see page 156), and crumbs; and fried in deep fat (300°F.) until brown. This is the way Bookbinder's usually serves it. The cakes can also be sautéed in butter.

CRABMEAT DEWEY A LA BOOKBINDER

1 pound lump crabmeat
6 tablespoons butter
2 tablespoons chopped green pepper
½ pound mushrooms, sliced
1 pimiento, chopped
2 tablespoons flour
1 cup heavy cream
¼ cup sherry

Sauté crabmeat in 4 tablespoons butter until heated through. Meanwhile, sauté green pepper, mushrooms, and pimiento in the remaining 2 tablespoons butter until soft. Add flour and mix in well. Add cream and stir constantly until thickened. Add sautéed crabmeat and sherry. Be sure that all is piping hot, but do not boil. Serve on toast or in patty shells.

Serves 4.

IMPERIAL CRAB

¼ cup butter
¼ cup flour
1 cup milk
　Salt and pepper
¼ cup diced green pepper
2 pimientos, diced
½ teaspoon Worcestershire sauce
　Drop of Tabasco sauce
2 tablespoons minced parsley
2 pounds crabmeat
2 egg yolks, well beaten

Melt butter, add flour, and stir until smooth. Add milk and continue cooking over medium heat, stirring constantly, until thickened. Add the rest of the ingredients and mix well. Continue cooking until heated through, but do not boil. Put into 8 individual casseroles or shells and brown under the broiler.

Serves 8.

LOBSTER IMPERIAL

Follow recipe for Imperial Crab, substituting lobster meat for the crabmeat.

SCALLOPS IMPERIAL

Follow recipe for Imperial Crab, substituting scallops for the crabmeat.

CRAB RAVIGOTTE

    1½ pounds crabmeat
      2 tablespoons chopped green pepper
      2 pimientos, chopped
     ¼ cup finely chopped celery
      1 cup mayonnaise
      2 hard-cooked egg yolks, grated
      6 strips pimiento
      6 strips green pepper
         Black olives
         Stuffed green olives } for garnish
         Lettuce
         Parsley

Mix the crabmeat, chopped green pepper, pimientos, celery and ¾ cup mayonnaise. Pile into six shells, mounding the mixture neatly. Cover thinly with remaining mayonnaise. Sprinkle with grated egg yolk. Decorate each with a pimiento strip and a green pepper strip. Garnish the plates upon which the crab is served with black olives, stuffed green olives, lettuce, parsley.

    Serves 6.

SAUTEED CRABMEAT

      1 pound lump crabmeat
     ½ stick sweet butter
      1 teaspoon paprika
         Salt and pepper

Melt sweet butter in skillet. Add paprika and cook until brown. Add lump crabmeat and salt and pepper to taste. When the crabmeat is golden brown on one side, turn and brown other side. Serve on slices of toast.

Serves 3.

CRABMEAT A LA NEWBURG

> 2 cups canned or fresh cooked crabmeat
> 2 tablespoons butter
> Salt to taste
> Cayenne pepper to taste
> 1 teaspoon paprika
> 4 egg yolks
> 1 cup light cream
> ½ cup dry sherry
> 1 tablespoon brandy, if desired

Melt butter in top of a double boiler over hot, not boiling water; add salt, cayenne pepper, and paprika. Beat egg yolks; add cream and sherry, and beat again to blend thoroughly. Slowly add egg yolk mixture to melted butter. Cook, stirring constantly, until thickened. Add crabmeat and continue cooking until crabmeat is heated through. Blend in brandy, if desired, and serve on toast points.

Serves 6.

LOBSTER A LA NEWBURG

Follow the recipe for Crabmeat à la Newburg, substituting lobster for the crabmeat.

SHRIMP A LA NEWBURG

Follow the recipe for Crabmeat à la Newburg, substituting shrimp for the crabmeat.

STUFFED CRAB

> 1 pound cooked crabmeat
> 1 tablespoon butter
> 1 small onion, chopped
> 2 hard-cooked eggs, chopped
>   Pinch thyme
> 1 teaspoon freshly chopped parsley
> 1 bay leaf
> 1 clove garlic, mashed (if desired)
>   Salt and pepper
>   Cayenne pepper
>   Buttered bread crumbs
>   Paprika

Pick over crabmeat carefully to remove any bony fibers. Melt butter in a skillet. Add chopped onion and cook over low heat until onion is soft, but not brown. Mix crabmeat, chopped eggs, thyme, parsley, bay leaf, and garlic (optional). Season with salt, pepper, and cayenne pepper to taste. Add to sautéed onion, blending thoroughly, and cook for 5 minutes. Remove bay leaf. Place mixture in ramekins, sprinkle buttered bread crumbs over the tops, and dust with paprika. Bake in a hot (400°F.) oven for 5 minutes or until nicely browned.
Serves 4.

SOFT-SHELL CRABS SAUTE

    12 small soft-shell crabs
       Salt and pepper
       Flour
    ¼ cup butter
    ¼ cup vegetable oil
       Lemon juice

Have the fish dealer clean your crabs. Season the crabs with salt and pepper and dip them into flour. Heat butter and oil together and sauté crabs in the mixture until golden brown. To serve, pour the juices from the pan over the crabs and add a squeeze of lemon juice.

    Serves 4.

Note: Sautéed crabs may also be served with lightly sautéed, slivered, blanched almonds sprinkled over them.

FRIED SOFT-SHELL CRABS

    12 small soft-shell crabs
       Salt and pepper
       Flour
       Egg Batter (see page 156)
       Fine bread or corn-flake crumbs
       Tartare Sauce (see page 153)

Have the fish dealer clean your crabs. Season the crabs and dip them into flour, then Egg Batter, then crumbs. Fry in deep fat

(375°F.) 6 to 8 minutes until nicely browned. Serve with Tartare Sauce.

Serves 4.

FROG'S LEGS SAUTE

2 pairs large or 3 pairs small frog's legs per person
Flour
Salt and pepper
Paprika
Half butter, half olive oil for frying
Lemon wedges
Tartare Sauce (see page 153)

Season flour with salt, pepper, and paprika. Coat frog's legs well with the seasoned flour and fry in mixed butter and oil 5 minutes at fairly high heat to brown quickly. They must not be over-cooked, as they are very delicate. Serve with lemon wedges and Tartare Sauce.

BAKED LOBSTER

4 1-pound fresh lobsters
2 cups corn-flake crumbs
Salt and pepper
¼ cup melted butter
¼ cup milk
¼ cup dry sherry
1 pound fresh crabmeat
Melted butter

Split and clean lobster (or have your fish dealer do this for you and hurry home to cook them); remove stomachs and back veins, leaving all fat, tomalley, and juice. Make stuffing as follows: Mix crumbs with salt, pepper, melted butter, milk, and dry sherry. Stir in crabmeat and mound mixture on top of lobsters. Pour melted butter over all. Bake in a hot (400°F.) oven for 10 to 12 minutes.

Serves 4.

BOILED LOBSTER

> 4 live lobsters
> ½ cup diced celery
> 1 onion, peeled
>   Drawn butter
>   Lemon wedges

Place lobsters in a kettle of briskly boiling salted water to cover. Add celery and onion. Cover and bring back to boiling. Boil rapidly, covered, 6 to 8 minutes for 1½-pound lobsters. Remove from water, drain well, place each on its back and split down the body lengthwise. Remove stomach and intestinal vein. Serve with drawn butter and lemon wedges.

Serves 4.

BROILED LOBSTER

Lobster must be alive!

Turn the lobster on its back and split from tail to head. Remove stomach, located at the head. Remove the long vein which runs

the length of the lobster. Brush the flesh with melter butter and
sprinkle with paprika. Place 6 inches from the broiler heat and
broil as follows:

1¼-pound lobster	15 minutes
1½- to 3-pound lobster	25 minutes
3- to 4-pound lobster	30 minutes

Note: It is very hard, particularly for a woman, to split a lobster.
So, despite the admonition above to the effect that the lobster
must be alive, I will tell you that my system is to go to the fish
market as near cooking time as I can, get the market man to
split my lobsters for me, dash home and cook them as above.
It may not be proper, but it's much easier!

BROILED LOBSTER, MAINE STYLE

      4 1½- to 2-pound lobsters
   1½ cups cracker crumbs
     ½ teaspoon salt
      1 tablespoon Worcestershire sauce
      4 tablespoons melted butter
          Drawn butter

Either split the lobsters or have it done at the market. Remove
intestinal vein, stomach, and liver. Mix the liver with cracker
crumbs, salt, Worcestershire sauce, and melted butter. Spread
this dressing generously in the cavity from which liver and stomach were removed. Cut off four of the small claws from each
lobster and press these into the dressing. Place the lobsters on a
greased tray and bake 8 minutes in a moderate (375°F.) oven.

Remove from oven and place 6 inches from heat in 450°F. broiler (about 6 minutes). Serve with drawn butter.

Serves 4.

CURRIED LOBSTER

- 4 tablespoons butter
- 3 tablespoons flour
- 1 tablespoon curry powder (or more, to taste)
- 1 cup Fish Stock (see page 154)
- 1 cup light cream
  Salt and pepper to taste
- 2 cups cooked lobster meat

Melt butter. Blend flour and curry powder into the butter, stirring until smooth. Cook over medium heat for 5 minutes. Add stock and cream; stir constantly until thickened. Season with salt and pepper to taste. Add lobster and allow to heat through. Serve on dry rice.

Serves 4 to 6.

Note: This same recipe may be used for crabmeat, shrimp, or a mixture of seafoods.

FRIED LOBSTER

- 1 pound cooked lobster meat, cut in large pieces
  Flour
  Salt and pepper
- 1 egg, slightly beaten with a little milk
  Bread crumbs
  Deep fat for frying

Mix flour, salt, and pepper. Roll the lobster pieces in the mixture, then dip in beaten egg and milk. Roll in bread crumbs. Fry in deep hot (375°F.) fat until golden brown.

Serves 2 to 3.

LOBSTER MONTE CARLO

> 2 cups diced lobster meat
> 4 tablespoons Worcestershire sauce
> ½ cup grated sharp cheese
> ¼ cup dry bread crumbs
> ¼ cup melted butter

Warm the lobster meat in top of a double boiler. Put into four individual shallow flameproof dishes. Sprinkle Worcestershire sauce over the lobster. Mix grated cheese and bread crumbs and top each dish with them. Sprinkle melted butter over the tops and place under the broiler to brown.

Serves 4.

STEAMED LOBSTER

What we are accustomed to calling "boiled" lobster is cooked, at Bookbinder's, in huge steam pressure cookers, some of which have sat under the front windows since the restaurant was opened. Mr. Taxin at first told me that cooking under pressure is the only possible method for achieving the succulent goodness of the lobsters served at Bookbinder's, but we finally compromised on a recipe for boiling them.

I was, however, thoroughly challenged by the pressure method and finally tried it in a pressure canner, since the average home pressure cooker would obviously not be big enough to hold one lobster, let alone enough for several people. If you have a pressure canner, which we'll admit not many people have, you can do absolutely wonderful "boiled" lobsters in it. Put them in with very little water, bring the pressure up to 15 pounds, and cook for 6 minutes. This is for 1½-pound lobsters. Cook a little longer for heavier ones. Remove when the steam has gone down. Split and serve at once with drawn butter.

LOBSTER THERMIDOR BOOKBINDER

        2 2½-pound lobsters
        2 cups tomato sauce
      ¼ cup tomato purée
        2 tablespoons powdered chicken base
        1 teaspoon Worcestershire sauce
        1 bay leaf
        2 cloves
      , 2 whole allspice
      ¼ teaspoon nutmeg
        1 veal bone
        1 onion, chopped
        3 stalks celery, chopped
           Salt and white pepper, to taste
        3 tablespoons butter
        2 tablespoons flour
        1 tablespoon cornstarch
           Grated Parmesan cheese

Boil or steam lobsters. When cool enough to handle, split, remove meat, and dice it. Reserve the four half-shells. Place tomato sauce and all remaining ingredients except butter, flour, and cornstarch in a saucepan and simmer gently for an hour. Remove veal bone and bay leaf. Press remainder through a sieve or whirl in the blender. Melt butter, add flour and cornstarch, and stir until smooth. Add a little of the tomato mixture and stir until smooth. Add to remainder of the tomato mixture and stir to blend well. Place lobster meat in sauce. Fill into lobster shell halves, top with grated Parmesan cheese and broil, 3 inches from heat, 5 minutes or until golden.

Serves 4.

BROILED OYSTERS

24 oysters with liquor
Salt
Paprika
Butter

Place oysters on a large tray which will fit into your broiler. Sprinkle with salt and paprika and dot generously with butter. Broil 3 inches from heat at 375°F. until edges of oysters curl (3 to 4 minutes). Serve on toast.

Serves 4.

BROILED OYSTERS A LA BOOKBINDER

    12 oysters on half shell
       Rock salt
     1 large mushroom, chopped fine
     1 teaspoon minced onion
     1 tablespoon butter
       Flour for dredging
    ½ cup warm milk
    ¼ cup cooked oatmeal
       Salt and pepper
     1 tablespoon minced parsley
     3 tablespoons grated Parmesan cheese
     2 tablespoons melted butter

Sauté mushroom and onion in 1 tablespoon butter until soft, but not brown (about 10 minutes). Dredge with flour and stir to blend smoothly. Add milk and stir until thickened. Add oatmeal and stir well. Season to taste with salt and pepper; stir in parsley. Place oysters on rock salt (enough to hold them in place) in tray. Put under 400°F. broiler heat for 4 minutes. Remove from broiler and cover each with sauce. Sprinkle each oyster with Parmesan cheese and a few drops of melted butter. Return to the broiler and cook until golden brown (about 5 minutes).
    Serves 2.

CREAMED OYSTERS WITH TRIPE

     1 pound honeycomb tripe
    16 oysters with liquor
     2 cups tripe stock and oyster liquor

4 tablespoons butter
4 tablespoons flour
  Salt and pepper
  Paprika

Cut the tripe into narrow strips. Cover with boiling, salted water and cook, covered, at a simmer for 2 to 3 hours, or until tender. Drain, reserving stock. Cook oysters in their own liquor until they curl. Drain, reserving liquor. Pour remaining oyster liquor into a cup and add enough tripe stock to make 2 cups. Melt butter and blend in flour, stirring until smooth. Add tripe stock and oyster liquor and stir constantly until thickened. Season to taste with salt and pepper. Add tripe and oysters and heat through. Serve on toast, sprinkled with paprika.

Serves 4.

FRIED OYSTERS

1 quart oysters
  Egg Batter (see page 156)
  Dry bread or corn-flake crumbs
  Tartare Sauce (see page 153)

Drain oysters well. Dip into batter, then into crumbs. Fry in deep fat (375°F.) until delicately brown (about 2 minutes). Do not do too many at a time because if they touch they are likely to lose their coating. Serve with Tartare Sauce, or with chicken salad in the Bookbinder manner.

OYSTER AND HAM TURNOVERS

4 tablespoons butter
4 tablespoons flour
1 cup milk
1 teaspoon Worcestershire sauce
½ teaspoon salt
  Dash of freshly ground pepper
1 cup chopped boiled ham
8 large oysters, chopped
1 recipe pastry (using 2 cups flour)
  Oyster Sauce I (see page 151)

Melt butter; add flour and stir until smooth. Add milk and cook over medium heat, stirring constantly, until thick. Add Worcestershire sauce, salt, and pepper. Add the chopped ham and oysters. Roll out chilled pastry and cut into 6-inch circles. Place about 2 tablespoons of the ham and oyster mixture in the center of each pastry circle. Fold over and seal the edges of the pastry. Prick the top with the tines of a fork to allow steam to escape. Bake in a hot (425°F.) oven 25 minutes or until golden brown. Remove to a rack for a few minutes, to set. Serve hot with Oyster Sauce I.

Makes 8 turnovers.

OYSTERS IN PAPER

36 oysters, with their liquid
   Salt and pepper
 2 tablespoons sherry

2 tablespoons finely chopped onion
Capers
2 tablespoons chopped chives
2 tablespoons chopped celery leaves

Place six freshly opened oysters and their liquid on a square of aluminum foil. Season with salt and pepper, 1 teaspoon sherry, 1 teaspoon onion, a few capers, 1 teaspoon chives and 1 teaspoon celery leaves. Bring edges of foil together and fold securely so that none of the juices will come out during baking. Follow these directions for remaining oysters. Bake in a hot (400°F.) oven for 12 minutes. Remove bundles. Turn contents onto freshly made toast spread with anchovy butter, or serve bundles unopened and let each diner open his own.

Serves 6.

OYSTERS PHILADELPHIA

12 to 16 medium-sized oysters on the half shell
4 tablespoons sherry
Rock salt
¼ cup finely chopped celery
1 tablespoon butter
Béchamel Sauce (see page 145)
Paprika
Grated Parmesan cheese
Melted butter

Poach oysters in their own liquor for 2 minutes. Sprinkle sherry over them. Clean the bottom of the deeper oyster shells and set them on a baking tray covered with rock salt. Sauté chopped celery in butter and place 1 teaspoonful in each shell. Place a poached oyster on each bed of celery and cover with Béchamel Sauce which has been mixed with a little paprika and grated Parmesan cheese. Sprinkle a few drops of melted butter over each oyster. Bake in a hot (400°F.) oven until golden brown. Serve with dark bread and butter.

Serves 2.

SCALLOPED OYSTERS

    1 quart oysters
    4 tablespoons oyster liquor
    ½ cup soft bread crumbs
    ½ cup cracker crumbs
    ½ cup melted butter
    2 tablespoons milk or cream
    ½ teaspoon salt
    ¼ teaspoon pepper

Drain oysters, reserving 4 tablespoons liquor. Carefully remove any bits of shell from the oysters. Mix together bread and cracker crumbs; stir in melted butter. Blend oyster liquor, milk, salt, and pepper. Place a thin layer of the buttered crumbs on the bottom of a shallow 8-inch square baking dish, then a layer of oysters, and sprinkle with oyster liquor. Repeat layering until all ingredients are used, ending with crumbs. Bake in a hot (400°F.) oven 30 minutes or until golden.

Serves 4.

SHIRRED OYSTERS

    6 oysters with liquor
      Cream
    2 teaspoons butter
    2 teaspoons flour
      Salt and pepper
      Bread crumbs
      Butter for dotting

Put oysters into a shallow, broiler-proof dish with their liquor
and cook over medium heat until edges curl. Remove oysters.
Pour remaining oyster liquor into a cup and add enough cream
to make ½ cupful. Melt butter and blend in flour, stirring until
smooth. Add cream and oyster liquor and stir until thickened.
Season to taste with salt and pepper and add oysters. Sprinkle
bread crumbs over and dot with butter. Place in broiler until nicely
browned.
      Serves 1.

BAKED SCALLOPS

    1½ pounds scallops
       Flour
       Light cream
       Butter for dotting
       Salt and pepper

If any of the scallops are too large, cut them in half. Roll in flour
and place in a greased pan so that each stands separately by itself—no layers. Pour in light cream to come just halfway up the

depth of the scallops. Dot with butter and season with salt and pepper. Bake in a moderate (350°F.) oven 25 to 30 minutes.

Serves 4.

BROILED SCALLOPS

> 1 pound scallops
> Salt and pepper
> Paprika
> Butter

Place scallops on shallow tray or pie plates. Sprinkle with salt, pepper, and paprika. Dot with butter. Broil 3 inches from the heat 6 to 8 minutes, or until the scallops are very delicately browned.

Serves 2 to 3.

FRIED SCALLOPS

> 1½ pounds scallops
> Flour
> Salt and pepper
> Paprika
> Egg Batter (see page 156)
> Seasoned flour and bread crumbs (half and half)
> Tartare Sauce (see page 153)

If any of the scallops are too large, cut them in half. Roll in flour seasoned with salt, pepper, and paprika. Dip into batter then roll in mixture of seasoned flour and bread crumbs. Fry in deep fat, 375°F., 4 minutes, or until golden brown. Put only a single layer

in the frying basket at one time so that all will be evenly browned.
Serve with Tartare Sauce.

Serves 4.

FRIED SCALLOPS DELMONICO

2 pounds scallops
1 egg, beaten
3 tablespoons chopped ham
4 tablespoons bread crumbs
2 tablespoons grated Parmesan cheese
1 tablespoon chopped chives
   Tartare Sauce (see page 153)

Mix together all ingredients except scallops. Dip scallops in mixture. Place in a wire basket and fry in deep hot (385°F.) fat until crisply brown. Serve with Tartare Sauce.

Serves 4 to 6.

SCALLOP SALAD

2 pounds scallops
1 quart boiling water
1 tablespoon lemon juice
½ tablespoon salt
1 cup mayonnaise
1 cup diced celery
¼ cup chopped sweet pickles
   Lettuce

Add scallops to boiling water to which lemon juice and salt have been added. Cook until the scallops are done, about 5 minutes. Drain well. Chill and cut in cubes. Add mayonnaise, celery, and sweet pickles and mix lightly. Chill for 1 hour and serve on lettuce cups.

Serves 6.

BOILED SHRIMP

Wash the shrimp in cold water and drop into rapidly boiling, salted water. Cover tightly and cook for 5 minutes. Drain and cover with cold water to chill; then drain, remove shells and vein; prepare as desired. You may also cook shrimp in sieved sea water or Fish Stock (see page 154).

One pound fresh shrimp yields about 2 cups cooked, shelled shrimp.

SHRIMP COOKED IN BEER

    1 pound uncooked fresh shrimp
    1½ cups beer

Wash, shell, and devein shrimp. Bring the beer to a boil; add shrimp. Reduce heat and cook the shrimp over low heat 5 minutes. Remove shrimp from beer, allow to cool, and chill.

SHRIMP AU GRATIN

    2 cups chopped cooked shrimp
    ¼ cup butter

¼ cup flour
2 cups light cream
1 cup grated Cheddar cheese
Salt and pepper
¼ cup bread crumbs
Butter for dotting

Melt butter; add flour and stir until smooth. Add light cream and cook over medium heat, stirring constantly, until thickened. Add half of the grated Cheddar cheese and stir to blend thoroughly. Season to taste with salt and pepper. Stir in the shrimp. Place in one large casserole or in individual baking dishes. Cover with remaining grated cheese, mixed with bread crumbs. Dot with butter. Bake in a hot (400°F.) oven 20 to 25 minutes, or until delicately browned.

Serves 4.

SCAMPI BOOKBINDER

3 pounds shelled uncooked shrimp
½ cup olive oil
Salt and pepper
4 cloves garlic, finely chopped
½ cup finely chopped parsley

Wash and dry shrimp. Sauté shrimp in hot oil for 5 minutes. Remove to hot serving platter and season with salt and pepper. Add chopped garlic and parsley to oil remaining in pan and cook for 1 minute. Pour this sauce over the shrimp and serve immediately.

Serves 6.

Note: Lobster meat or lobster tails may be used instead of shrimp.

SHRIMP CROQUETTES

2 cups finely chopped cooked shrimp
1 cup thick white sauce
1 tablespoon sherry
  Flour
  Egg Batter (see page 156)
  Corn-flake crumbs
  Shrimp Newburg Sauce (see page 152)

Combine the shrimp, white sauce, and sherry; mix well and place in refrigerator to chill thoroughly. Form into croquettes. Dip in flour, then in batter, then in crumbs; fry in deep fat (375°F.) until nicely browned. Serve with Shrimp Newburgh Sauce.
  Serves 4.

Note: Lobster croquettes are made in this same fashion. Serve with Lobster Newburg Sauce (see page 153).

SHRIMP CUTLET

4 pounds cooked, diced shrimp
1 green pepper, chopped
1 medium onion, chopped
¼ pound butter
½ cup flour
1 tablespoon salt
½ teaspoon pepper
2 eggs
¼ cup dry sherry

Flour
Bread crumbs

Sauté chopped pepper and onion in butter until soft but not brown. Remove from heat. Add ½ cup flour and blend thoroughly. Season with salt and pepper. Combine 1 egg and the dry sherry, beat well, and add to pepper and onion mixture. When all is blended, add shrimp. Chill for at least 1 hour. Shape shrimp mixture into cutlets. Beat remaining egg slightly. Dip the cutlets into flour, then into beaten egg, and then into crumbs. Fry in deep hot (350°F.) fat until golden brown. Turn while frying to brown all sides.

Serves 8.

FRIED SHRIMP

½ cup flour
¼ teaspoon salt
1 egg, slightly beaten
⅓ cup milk
2 dozen shrimp, shelled and cleaned
Lemon wedges
Tartare Sauce (see page 153)

Sift together flour and salt. Add egg and milk and beat until smooth. Dip shrimp into batter and fry in deep hot (365°F.) fat until golden brown. Turn while frying to brown all sides. Serve with lemon wedges and Tartare Sauce.

Serves 4.

FRIED BUTTERFLY SHRIMP

1½ pounds shrimp
     Flour
     Egg Batter (see page 156)
     Bread or corn-flake crumbs
     Tartare Sauce (see page 153)
     Lemon wedges

Shell and clean shrimp, leaving the tails on. Split them down the back, being very careful not to cut through the other side. Flatten them out. Dip into flour, then batter, then crumbs. Fry in deep fat (375°F.) until nicely browned. Serve with Tartare Sauce and lemon wedges.
Serves 4.

SHRIMP DU JOUR

 3 pounds uncooked shrimp, shelled
¼ pound butter
 2 teaspoons Worcestershire sauce
 1 clove garlic, chopped
¼ cup chopped chives
¼ cup chopped parsley
    Salt and pepper
    Grated cheese
    Bread crumbs
    Drawn butter

Sauté shrimp in butter with Worcestershire sauce, garlic, chives, parsley, salt, and pepper for 5 minutes. Place in a large casserole and sprinkle with grated cheese and bread crumbs. Pour butter in which shrimp were cooked over all. Bake in a hot (400°F.) oven for about 8 to 10 minutes or until golden brown. Serve with drawn butter.

Serves 6.

STUFFED SHRIMP

        8 jumbo shrimp
        2 tablespoons butter
        2 tablespoons flour
        ½ cup milk
     1¼ cups lump crabmeat
        1 teaspoon salt
          White pepper to taste
          Flour for dipping
          Egg Batter (see page 156)
          Bread or corn-flake crumbs

Shell and clean the shrimp. Split down the back, being very careful not to cut through the other side. Melt butter. Blend in 2 tablespoons flour, stirring until smooth. Add milk and stir until thickened. Mix with crabmeat. Season with salt and pepper. Divide crabmeat mixture into 8 equal portions and mold one portion onto each shrimp, pressing firmly with the hand. Dip stuffed shrimp into flour, then batter, then crumbs. Fry in deep fat (375°F.) until delicately brown (8 to 10 minutes).

Serves 4.

SHRIMP SUPREME

> 1 pound uncooked jumbo shrimp
> Bacon slices
> Egg Batter (see page 156)
> Bread crumbs

Wash, shell, and devein shrimp. Cut bacon strips in half cross-wise and then in half again lengthwise. Split each shrimp, open flat, and wrap a piece of bacon around each. Tuck ends of bacon slices under so that they do not come out during cooking. Dip wrapped shrimp in batter, and then in crumbs. Fry in deep (350°F.) fat until golden brown, about 10 minutes.

Serves 2.

Fish

BAKED FISH

If you're baking fish without a sauce add a bit of Fish Stock (see page 154) to provide moisture and help prevent sticking. Bake fish from 8 to 12 minutes per pound, depending upon thickness and type of fish. The fish is done when it flakes easily with a fork.

BROILED FISH

When you broil any fish, whether steaks, a split whole fish, or fillets, salt and pepper it well and dot it generously with butter. As with all fish cookery, your chief concern should be not to overcook the fish. This means, for instance, that when you have a thick split shad to cook (which you will cook flesh side up and *not* turn) it may take 8 to 12 minutes to cook, whereas a thin fillet will be done in 5 minutes with one turning. It's a good idea to keep basting fish while it's broiling, too, to prevent it from drying out.

FISH NORFOLK, BOOKBINDER STYLE

    1½ cups cooked flaked fish (haddock, finnan haddie, codfish, or halibut)
    2 hard-cooked eggs

¼ teaspoon paprika
   Dash of celery salt
   Salt
¼ pound fat salt pork, diced
 2 cups hot, cooked rice
   Minced parsley (optional)

Separate the whites from the yolks of the hard-cooked eggs. Rice the egg yolks and set aside. Chop the egg whites and add the fish, paprika, celery salt, and salt to taste. Try out the pork until the cracklings are crisp. Add fish mixture and toss well with a fork until heated through. Pile the rice on a serving dish, cover with the fish and garnish with the riced egg yolks and with minced parsley, if desired.

Serves 4.

THREE-WAY FISH PIE

 1 small onion, peeled
 1 carrot
 1 stalk celery
   Salt and pepper
1½ pounds halibut
 1 chicken bouillon cube
 2 tablespoons butter
 1 tablespoon chopped onion
 2 tablespoons flour
 1 teaspoon chopped parsley
½ pound cooked shrimp
½ pound cooked scallops
   Rich pie crust

Boil whole peeled onion, carrot, celery stalk, salt, and pepper in 1 quart water. After boiling 10 minutes, reduce heat, add halibut, cover, and simmer until tender. Remove skin and bones, place fish on a hot plate, and return skin and bones to the bouillon. Cook 15 minutes longer, then add the bouillon cube. Strain and reserve this stock.

Melt butter in a pan, add chopped onion, and sauté several minutes over low heat. Stir in flour slowly. When well blended, pour in 2¼ cups of the strained stock. Add parsley and season to taste with salt and pepper. Break fish into large pieces and place in a deep, greased baking dish, alternating with the cooked shrimp and scallops. Pour the sauce over all and cover with pastry. Make several incisions in crust. Bake 12 minutes in a very hot oven (450°F.), then reduce heat to 350°F, and bake 20 minutes longer.

Serves 6 generously.

FRESH COD AU GRATIN

    2 cups cooked fresh cod, flaked
    ¼ cup butter
    ¼ cup flour
    2 cups light cream
    1 cup grated Cheddar cheese
      Salt and pepper
    ¼ cup bread crumbs
      Butter for dotting

Melt butter, add flour, and stir until smooth. Add cream and cook over medium heat, stirring constantly, until thickened. Add ½ cup grated Cheddar cheese and stir to blend thoroughly. Season to taste with salt and pepper. Stir in the fish lightly, so as not to break it up too much. Put in a baking dish. Combine remaining ½ cup grated cheese with bread crumbs and sprinkle over the fish. Dot with butter. Bake in a hot (400°F.) oven 20 to 25 minutes, or until delicately browned.

Serves 4.

CODFISH CAKES A LA BOOKBINDER

> 1 pound codfish
> Salt
> 1 small onion, peeled
> 2 stalks celery
> 1 cup mashed potatoes
> 2 tablespoons melted butter
> 1 egg, well beaten
> 2 tablespoons finely chopped parsley
> Flour
> Egg Batter (see page 156)
> Fine bread or corn-flake crumbs
> Tomato Sauce (see page 153)

Wrap codfish in cheesecloth and steam in a very small amount of water seasoned with salt and celery leaves. When fish flakes easily with a fork, drain and carefully remove any bones. Put fish, onion, and celery stalks through the meat grinder. Mix with mashed potatoes, melted butter, beaten egg, and chopped parsley. Form into cakes. Chill well. Dip into flour, then batter, then crumbs. Fry in deep fat until golden. *Or,* dip into flour only and sauté in butter until golden. Serve with Tomato Sauce.

Serves 4.

BROILED FINNAN HADDIE

> 2 pounds finnan haddie
> Butter
> Paprika
> Fresh-ground pepper

Steam the finnan haddie in very little water about 15 minutes. Drain. Remove center bone and place the fish in a shallow baking tray. Dot with butter and sprinkle with paprika. Add fresh-ground pepper to taste. Broil 3 inches from heat about 5 minutes.
Serves 4.

CREAMED FINNAN HADDIE

> 1½ pounds finnan haddie
> 4 tablespoons butter
> 4 tablespoons flour
> 2 cups light cream
> Salt and fresh-ground pepper

Steam the fish in very little water until it flakes easily. Drain and flake. Melt the butter. Blend in flour, stirring until smooth. Add cream and continue cooking over medium heat, stirring constantly until thickened. Season to taste with salt and pepper. Add finnan haddie and heat through. Serve on toast.
Serves 4.

FINNAN HADDIE CASSEROLE

1 finnan haddie fillet (1 to 1½ pounds)
Skim milk to cover
2 tablespoons butter
1 small green pepper, diced
1 medium onion, diced
4 tablespoons flour
Dash of salt
2½ cups scalded milk
Paprika
Buttered bread crumbs

Cut the fish into three or four pieces. Place in a saucepan and cover with skim milk. Place over low heat and simmer about ½ hour, or until fish will flake easily with a fork. Meanwhile, melt butter and simmer diced green pepper and onion in it until soft, but not brown (about 10 minutes). Add flour and stir until the mixture is smooth and well blended. Add salt and scalded milk; cook over medium heat, stirring constantly, until thickened. Drain and flake the fish and place it in a casserole. Pour the sauce over, sprinkle with paprika and buttered crumbs, and bake in a hot (400°F.) oven 10 minutes.

Serves 4.

FLOUNDER STUFFED WITH CRABMEAT

    1 pound flounder fillets
      Salt and pepper
      Butter for dotting
    ½ pound lump crabmeat
    ¼ cup melted butter
      Dash of cayenne pepper

Try to get your fillets in two pieces. Place in a greased shallow tray. Season with salt and pepper and dot generously with butter. Broil 3 inches from heat for 3 minutes. Meanwhile, mix crabmeat with melted butter, salt, pepper, and cayenne pepper to taste. Remove fillets from broiler. Turn one over and cover it with the crabmeat mixture. Top with the other fillet, browned side up. Dot with more butter and bake 10 minutes in a moderate (350°F.) oven.
    Serves 2.

HADDOCK FILLETS WITH OYSTER STUFFING

    6 large oysters, chopped
    ½ cup dried bread crumbs
    2 tablespoons chopped celery
    ½ teaspoon salt
      Dash of freshly ground pepper
    2 tablespoons melted butter
    2 haddock fillets (about 2 pounds)
      Lemon juice
    4 thin slices salt pork
      Bread crumbs for sprinkling
      Oyster Sauce II (see page 151)

The easiest way to chop oysters is to put them into the blender with a little of their liquor and turn it on and almost immediately off. In any case, use a little liquor with the chopped ones, however you prepare them. Mix chopped oysters, crumbs, celery, seasonings, and melted butter. Place one fillet on a greased ovenproof pan. Sprinkle with salt and pepper. Spread oyster stuffing on top. Place second fillet on top. Sprinkle with salt, pepper, and lemon juice, then with bread crumbs. Place salt pork slices on top and bake in a moderate (375°F.) oven 25 to 35 minutes, or until pork is crisp and brown. Serve with Oyster Sauce II.

Serves 6.

Note: If you cannot get fresh haddock fillets, try this with halibut steaks. It is very good.

HADDOCK A LA RAREBIT

       1 3-pound haddock
       2 tablespoons butter
       2 heaping tablespoons flour
       1 heaping teaspoon dry mustard
     ½ teaspoon salt
          Freshly ground pepper
  1½ cups milk
       1 cup grated Cheddar cheese
          Paprika

Have the haddock skinned and boned. Put the fish into a flat, buttered baking dish. Melt the butter. Add flour and dry mustard and stir to make a smooth paste. Add salt, pepper, and milk. Cook over medium heat, stirring constantly until thickened. Add grated cheese and stir until it is melted and absorbed. Pour this sauce over the fish, sprinkle with paprika, and bake in a moderate (375°F.) oven 30 minutes.

Serves 6.

HALIBUT LOAF

> 2 cups cream
> 2½ cups soft bread crumbs
> 1 tablespoon butter
>   Salt and celery salt to taste
> 1 pound uncooked halibut
> 4 egg whites
>   Lobster Sauce (see page 149)

Scald cream. Add bread crumbs, butter, and seasonings. Put carefully boned uncooked halibut through the meat grinder, add to first mixture, and cook over medium heat until thoroughly heated. Beat egg whites until stiff and fold them into the fish mixture. Place in a greased casserole and set the casserole in a pan of hot water. Bake in a moderate (350°F.) oven about 1 hour, or until solid enough to slice, which you can test by inserting a flat knife. Serve sliced with Lobster Sauce.

Serves 6.

Note: Bookbinder's also makes this loaf with salmon in place of the halibut.

HALIBUT AU GRATIN

> 2 pounds halibut
> 2 teaspoons salt

2 tablespoons lemon juice
2 tablespoons butter
2 tablespoons flour
1½ cups scalded milk
1½ cups grated Cheddar cheese
    Salt and pepper
½ cup bread crumbs
    Paprika

Wrap halibut in cheesecloth and place in boiling water to cover entirely. Add salt and lemon juice. Bring back to boiling point, skim, and reduce heat at once. Cover and simmer about 20 minutes, or until fish flakes easily with a fork. Drain fish well, break it into pieces, and place the pieces in a baking dish. Melt the butter, blend in flour, and stir until smooth. Add scalded milk gradually, stirring until smooth. Add 1 cup grated cheese and continue cooking over medium heat, stirring constantly until sauce is thickened and smooth. Season to taste with salt and pepper. Pour the cheese sauce over the fish. Mix the remaining ½ cup of cheese with bread crumbs and sprinkle over the top of the dish. Top with a sprinkling of paprika. Bake in a moderate (350°F.) oven 30 minutes.

Serves 6.

OYSTER-STUFFED HALIBUT STEAK

        12 oysters
         1 cup cracker crumbs
         ½ teaspoon salt
            Fresh-ground pepper
         1 tablespoon chopped parsley
         2 tablespoons melted butter
         2 halibut steaks (about 1½ pounds each)
         1 tablespoon lemon juice
            Melted butter for basting
            Lemon slices

Drain oysters. Add crumbs, ½ teaspoon salt, pepper, parsley, and
2 tablespoons melted butter; mix well. Place one halibut steak
in a greased shallow baking dish. Sprinkle lemon juice over it
and season to taste with salt and pepper. Spread the oyster stuffing
over this and cover with the second steak. Fasten together with
small skewers or toothpicks. Brush with melted butter. Bake in
a moderate (350°F). oven 40 minutes, basting frequently with
more melted butter. Serve with slices of lemon.
    Serves 6.

FRESH BAKED LAKE TROUT

         1 3-pound trout
            Salt and white pepper
         3 tablespoons melted butter
         ½ cup bread crumbs
         2 teaspoons finely chopped tarragon

2 teaspoons finely chopped dill
2 teaspoons finely chopped parsley

Have trout split in half, and the bones and skin removed. Cut the fish into serving portions, place it in a greased baking dish, and sprinkle it with salt and white pepper. Pour melted butter over fish and scatter bread crumbs over the top. Bake in a moderate (350°F.) oven 30 minutes, or until fish flakes easily with a fork. Baste occasionally with extra melted butter. Ten minutes before the fish is to be done, sprinkle the herbs over it.

Serves 4 to 6.

BAKED STUFFED MACKEREL

1 large mackerel (2 to 3 pounds)
Salt
Plain Stuffing (see page 154)
Melted butter
Egg Sauce (see page 147)
Lemon slices

Rub the fish inside and out with salt. Stuff with Plain Stuffing. Fasten together with a skewer or sew up the opening. Brush with melted butter and place in a baking pan. Bake in a hot (450°F.) oven 15 minutes, basting frequently with melted butter. Reduce heat to 400°F. and bake 5 to 10 minutes longer, depending upon weight (allow a total baking time of about 10 minutes per pound). Serve with Egg Sauce and decorate with lemon slices.

Serves 4 to 6, depending upon weight of fish.

BAKED STUFFED SHAD

Follow recipe for Baked Stuffed Mackerel.

BROILED MACKEREL WITH MUSTARD PASTE

> 1 2-pound mackerel
> Salt and pepper
> 2 tablespoons butter
> Mustard-Parsley Paste (see below)
> 2 tablespoons lemon juice
> 1 lemon, sliced
> Parsley sprigs

Have fish split down the middle. Place the mackerel on a broiler pan, season with salt and pepper, and dot with butter. Broil, 2 to 3 inches from heat, 6 to 8 minutes. Remove from broiler and spread with Mustard-Parsley Paste. Place under the broiler again to melt the paste. Place fish on a hot platter and sprinkle the lemon juice over it. Garnish with lemon slices and sprigs of parsley.
Serves 4.

MUSTARD-PARSLEY PASTE

> 1 teaspoon prepared mustard
> 2 tablespoons butter
> 2 tablespoons finely chopped parsley
> 2 tablespoons lemon juice

Cream all together and spread on fish, as directed above.

POMPANO AMANDINE

> 2 pounds pompano fillets
> Salt and pepper
> Corn-flake crumbs
> ½ cup slivered blanched almonds
> Butter

Season the fillets with salt and pepper. Dip them into corn-flake crumbs and place in a well-greased shallow tray. Sprinkle the fillets with the almonds and dot generously with butter. Broil, 3 inches from heat, until fish flakes easily with a fork (4 to 6 minutes). Be careful not to overcook.

Serves 4.

COLD SALMON STEAK

> 1½ pounds salmon steaks (cut 1½ inches thick)
> 1 stalk celery with leaves, chopped
> 1 medium onion, chopped
> 1 teaspoon salt
> ½ teaspoon white pepper
> ¼ cup vinegar
> 2 tablespoons sugar
> 1 bay leaf
> 2 cloves

Place all ingredients in poacher and add just enough boiling water to cover the fish. Simmer for 20 minutes. Allow fish to cool in the stock. Leave the salmon in the stock and place it in the refrigerator to chill for at least 24 hours. Drain. Serve with

mayonnaise (pale green mayonnaise is particularly attractive).
Serves 4.

Note: Bookbinder's chefs say the longer this salmon sits in its
broth the better it tastes, but that doesn't mean indefinitely! Fish
is a perishable commodity.

SCROD

Bookbinder's serves scrod (which, as you doubtless know, is baby
cod) filleted and broiled (see page 82, Broiled Fish).

ROCKFISH

Bookbinder's serves big rockfish filleted and broiled, the small
ones split and broiled (see page 82, Broiled Fish).

PLANKED SHAD

At Bookbinder's, the fish is placed on oak boards; sprinkled with
salt, pepper, and paprika; dotted generously with butter; and
then cooked to perfection in a fireplace at the back of the restaurant's main room. At home, you can do a planked fish either
under the broiler or in the oven.

Oil the plank, which should have grooves for carrying the
juices into the deeper groove around the edge. Place the fish
on it, skin side down. Sprinkle with salt, pepper, and paprika,
and dot with butter. Place 3 inches from the broiler heat, or bake
in a hot (400°F.) oven. Baste with melted butter during the
cooking. Depending upon the thickness of the fish, it should take

8 to 12 minutes to cook. Five minutes before the fish is to be done, remove from broiler or oven and, using a pastry tube, pipe mashed potatoes around the fish, making a circle of the potato at one end. Return the fish to broiler or oven to brown the potato and finish cooking the fish. Before serving, fill the circle of potato with green peas.

PLANKED KING MACKEREL

Follow directions for Planked Shad.

BROILED SHAD ROE

    2 pair large shad roe
      Salt and pepper
      Butter

Steam shad roe until "set," about 8 minutes. Place on pan which will fit into your broiler. Sprinkle with salt and pepper and dot generously with butter. Broil under high heat, basting frequently with butter. Turn once to brown both sides. This should be done *fast* (not more than 2 minutes to a side), or the roe will become dry.
    Serves 4.

FRIED SMELTS

24 smelts
  Salted flour
  Corn-flake crumbs
4 tablespoons fat
  Tartare Sauce (see page 153)

Wipe smelts with a damp cloth. Roll them in salted flour, then in corn-flake crumbs. Fry the smelts in hot fat, turning them frequently, until they are golden brown (about 5 minutes). Serve with Tartare Sauce.

Serves 6.

SAUTEED SMELTS

Smelts should be split and cleaned, of course, but there is some disagreement about whether they should be decapitated before cooking. At Bookbinder's the heads are first removed. This is undoubtedly because many people faint at the very thought of seeing a fish with its head on presented upon a plate.

Dip the fish in flour and sauté in a combination of butter and oil—the butter is particularly for flavor, the oil because it doesn't burn as easily as the butter. The cooking should be quick, so a brisk heat is advised in order that the fish may brown nicely on both sides. This can be accomplished in 3 to 4 minutes.

BROILED SWORDFISH

2 pounds swordfish steak, cut 1-inch thick
Salt and pepper
Butter
½ cup Fish Stock (see page 154)
Anchovy Sauce (see page 144)

Place swordfish on a greased shallow tray which will fit into your broiler. Season with salt and pepper and dot with *plenty* of butter. Broil, 2 inches from heat, about 5 minutes. Add Fish Stock to pan and bake in a moderate (375°F.) oven for 5 minutes. Serve with Anchovy Sauce.
   Serves 4 to 6.

TROUT

Bookbinder's serves large trout filleted, either broiled or baked (see page 82). Small trout are dipped into flour, rolled in cornmeal and sautéed, whole.

WHITING IN CREOLE SAUCE

4 small whiting
1½ cups Creole Sauce (see page 146)

Have the whiting split and cleaned. Place the fish in a baking dish and pour Creole Sauce over it. Bake in a moderate (350°F.) oven about 10 minutes, or until the fish flake easily with a fork.
   Serves 4.

BROILED WHITING

>   4 small whiting
>   Salt and pepper
>   Melted butter

Have the whiting split and cleaned. Sprinkle with salt and pepper and brush with melted butter. Broil, about 4 inches from heat. until fish flake easily with a fork, basting frequently with more melted butter.

Serves 4.

Meats
and
Poultry

BOILED BEEF

4-pound eye-of-round roast
2 stalks celery, chopped
2 medium onions, peeled
2 medium carrots, quartered
1 clove garlic, peeled
2 teaspoons salt
Horseradish Sauce (see page 148)

Put meat and vegetables into a deep kettle. Add water to cover and the salt. Bring to boiling, then lower the heat and simmer 2 to 3 hours, or until tender. Drain well, reserving bouillon for future use. Serve meat, sliced, with Horseradish Sauce.

Serves 8 to 10.

BEEF POT PIES

1½ pounds beef chuck, cut in 1-inch cubes
Flour
Salt and pepper
2 tablespoons fat
1 tablespoon powdered beef stock
1 medium onion
1 bay leaf
½ cup diced celery

    2 medium onions, diced
    2 medium potatoes, diced
    ½ cup shelled peas
    4 tablespoons butter
    4 tablespoons flour
    2 cups beef stock
    Flaky pie crust

Dredge the beef cubes in flour seasoned with salt and pepper. Brown on all sides in hot fat. Cover with boiling water, add powdered beef stock, onion, and bay leaf, and simmer until tender (45 to 60 minutes). Cook the vegetables until they are just tender, and drain well. Arrange vegetables in four individual dishes. Melt the butter and blend in flour smoothly. Allow to brown. Add beef stock and stir constantly until thickened. Add cooked cubes of beef to this gravy and pour over the vegetables. Cover each dish with flaky pie crust, seal well at the edges, and prick the centers. Bake in a hot (400°F.) oven 15 to 20 minutes, or until the crust is nicely browned.

    Serves 4.

HUNGARIAN BEEF GOULASH

    1½ pounds chuck, cut in 2-inch chunks
    3 tablespoons butter
    Flour
    ½ cup chopped celery
    ½ cup chopped onions
    ½ cup chopped carrots
    1 clove garlic, mashed
    Salt and pepper
    1 tablespoon paprika

Brown meat chunks in butter. Dredge well with flour and let the flour brown, turning the meat frequently. Add vegetables and cover with water. Simmer, covered, 1½ to 2 hours, or until meat is tender. Season to taste with salt and pepper and mix the paprika in well. Cook 5 minutes longer.

Serves 4 to 6.

SPANISH MEAT LOAF

1½ pounds ground chuck
2 eggs
1 green pepper, minced
1 medium onion, minced
2 stalks celery, minced
1 clove garlic, crushed
  Salt and pepper
1 cup corn flakes
1 14-ounce bottle tomato catsup

Mix meat and eggs together well. Add all other ingredients except catsup and mix thoroughly. Press into meat loaf pan (9x5x2½ inches). Bake in a moderate (350°F.) oven ½ hour. Pour catsup over the loaf and bake for ½ hour more.

Serves 4 to 6.

PEPPER STEAK

1½ pounds chuck steak
  Flour
  Salt and pepper
4 tablespoons butter

½ cup sliced mushrooms
1 medium green pepper, sliced
½ cup bean sprouts
1 tablespoon soy sauce

Have the beef cut into long strips (like thin French-fried potatoes). Dredge with flour, season with salt and pepper, and brown
in the butter over high heat. Reduce heat, add mushrooms and
green pepper, cook over low heat until green pepper is soft (10
to 15 minutes). Add bean sprouts and soy sauce and simmer only
long enough to allow the bean sprouts to heat through. Correct
seasoning and serve on dry rice.

Serves 4.

STUFFED PEPPERS

4 green peppers
2 tablespoons minced onion
2 tablespoons minced celery
1 tablespoon butter
1 pound chopped chuck
2 cups cooked rice
1 tablespoon powdered beef stock
1 egg, beaten
¼ cup bread crumbs
¼ cup milk
Salt and pepper to taste

Cut off and discard tops of peppers. Cut the peppers in half
lengthwise and remove the seeds and membranes. Sauté onion
and celery in butter until soft, but not brown. Add chopped beef
and cook over medium heat, stirring constantly with a fork, until

red color disappears. Mix well with all other ingredients and stuff into pepper halves. Place in greased baking dish. Bake in a moderate (375°F.) oven 20 to 25 minutes.

Serves 4 or 8, depending upon appetites.

BOOKBINDER'S BRAISED SHORT RIBS

     4 pounds beef short ribs
       Salt and pepper
       Flour
   ½ cup diced celery
     1 clove garlic, mashed
     2 tablespoons chopped onion

Season the ribs with salt and pepper and dredge them lightly with flour. Place in a hot (450°F.) oven and brown well (about 15 minutes). Reduce heat to 350°F. Mix celery, garlic, and onion and spread the mixture over the meat. Add a little water to the pan and return it to the oven. Roast, basting occasionally and adding more water to the pan if necessary, for 1 hour, or until tender. Serve with pan gravy.

Serves 4.

SWISS STEAK

     2 pounds rump steak, ¼-inch thick
       Flour
       Salt and pepper
     2 tablespoons butter or bacon fat
     2 medium onions, sliced
   1½ cups beef stock

Pound the steak well. Dredge with flour and season with salt and pepper. In hot fat over high heat, brown the meat on all sides. The onions may be browned with the meat, or they may be added with the stock after the meat is browned. Reduce heat and simmer, covered, until meat is tender (1½ to 2 hours). If desired, thicken the gravy with butter and flour blended in equal quantities.

Serves 4 to 6.

Note: A crushed clove of garlic may be added when the meat is being browned.

PAN-BRAISED ENGLISH BEEF STEW

    2 pounds chuck, cut into 2-inch cubes
      Salt and pepper
      Flour
    2 tablespoons fat
    ½ cup diced celery
    ½ cup diced onion
    ½ cup diced carrots
    1 clove garlic, mashed
    2 cups stewed tomatoes
    2 cups shelled peas

Season meat with salt and pepper and dredge with flour. In a Dutch oven, brown the meat on all sides in the fat. Add all vegetables except peas and enough water to cover. Simmer gently until meat is tender (45 minutes to 1 hour). Fifteen minutes before the stew is to be done, add peas. Correct seasonings.

Serves 6.

CURRIED LAMB

        2 pounds boned shoulder of lamb
        2 medium onions, diced
    ½ cup diced celery
        1 clove garlic, crushed
        8 tablespoons (1 stick) butter
        3 tablespoons flour
        1 tablespoon curry powder (or more, to taste)
           Salt and pepper to taste

Have lamb diced in about 1¼-inch squares. Sauté the lamb, onion, celery, and garlic in 4 tablespoons (½ stick) butter until the meat is nicely browned. Cover with boiling, salted water and cook at a low boil for 30 minutes, or until meat is tender. Melt remaining ½ stick of butter and blend in the flour and curry powder, stirring until smooth. Cook over low heat, without browning, for 5 minutes. Add the stock from the lamb and stir constantly until thickened. Add lamb. Serve, piping hot, with dry rice and Major Grey's chutney.

    Serves 4 to 6.

Note: Major Grey's is a variety, not a brand, of Indian chutney.

LAMB PATTIES

        1 pound ground lamb
        1 egg
           Salt and pepper

½ cup bread crumbs
4 slices bacon
  Mushroom Sauce (see page 150)

Mix lamb, egg, seasonings, and bread crumbs. Form the mixture into 8 thin patties. Cut the bacon slices in half lengthwise and wrap one piece around each pattie; secure with a toothpick. Broil at 500°F. until bacon is crisp (10 to 15 minutes). Serve with Mushroom Sauce.

Serves 4.

PAN-BRAISED LAMB STEW

2 pounds neck or breast of lamb
  Salt and pepper
  Flour
½ cup diced celery
½ cup diced carrots
2 tablespoons minced onion
1 clove garlic, mashed
2 cups cooked green peas

Have the lamb cut into chunks. Season with salt and pepper and dredge lightly with flour. Place in a very hot (450°F.) oven and brown well (about 15 minutes). Reduce heat to 350°F. Put celery, carrots, onion, and garlic into the pan with the lamb and add a small amount (about ½ cup) of water. Return the lamb and vegetables to the oven and continue cooking, basting occasionally, for 1 hour, or until lamb is tender. Serve in casserole, topped with hot cooked green peas.

Serves 4.

BRAISED PORK CHOPS

    4 thick pork chops
    1 medium onion, sliced
    ¼ cup chopped celery
      Salt and pepper

Brown the pork chops in skillet without added fat. When they are brown, remove the chops from pan and brown the onion and celery in the same fat. Return the chops to the pan and add water to cover halfway up. Cover and simmer for 1 hour, turning the chops occasionally and adding more water if necessary. Season to taste with salt and pepper. The gravy may be thickened, if desired.

    Serves 4.

STUFFED PORK CHOPS

    4 thick pork chops, with pockets cut in the side
      Packaged poultry stuffing
      Salt and pepper

Have your butcher cut a pocket in the side of each chop. Prepare poultry stuffing according to package directions. Stuff pockets in chops with prepared poultry stuffing, fasten with skewers, and season chops with salt and pepper. Place the stuffed chops in a baking pan. Add a little water, just enough to keep the chops from sticking. Bake in a moderate (350°F.) oven for 1 hour, turning once and adding more water if necessary.

    Serves 4.

BRAISED HAM STEAK

1 ham steak, ¾-inch thick
1 cup canned crushed pineapple

In a skillet, brown the ham slice on both sides in its own fat. Pour the pineapple over the ham, cover, and simmer gently 25 to 30 minutes.

Serves 2 to 3.

BROILED HAM STEAK

1 ham steak, ½-inch thick
2 slices canned pineapple
  Pineapple juice

If the rind is still on the ham slice, cut it off and discard it. Make cuts in the fat around the edge of the slice to prevent it from curling. Broil at 350°F. 10 minutes. Turn, place pineapple slices on top of the ham and broil another 10 minutes. Baste occasionally with pineapple juice.

Serves 2 to 3.

CREAMED HAM

> 2 cups diced cooked ham
> 4 tablespoons butter
> 4 tablespoons flour
> 1 cup cream
> 1 cup veal or chicken stock
>   Salt and pepper
> 8 mushrooms, sliced and sautéed

Melt the butter. Add flour and blend until smooth. Add cream and stock; cook over medium heat, stirring constantly, until thickened. Season to taste with salt and pepper. Add ham and heat thoroughly. Add sautéed mushrooms and mix well.

Serves 4.

HAM CROQUETTES

> 2 cups ground ham
> 1 cup thick white sauce
> 2 teaspoons chopped parsley
>   Salt and pepper
>   Flour
>   Egg Batter (see page 156)
>   Bread or corn-flake crumbs

Mix together ham, white sauce, and parsley. Season to taste with salt and pepper. Chill the mixture thoroughly. Shape into croquettes, dip in flour, then in Egg Batter, then in crumbs. Fry in deep fat (375°F.) until nicely browned. Serve with scrambled eggs.

Serves 6.

BARBECUED SPARERIBS

4 pounds spareribs
2 cups tomato purée
¼ cup minced onion
¼ cup minced celery
1 tablespoon Worcestershire sauce
1 teaspoon dry mustard
  Tabasco sauce to taste
1 teaspoon sugar

Boil the spareribs in water to cover for ½ hour. Meanwhile, mix the rest of the ingredients and simmer gently together. When the spareribs have been boiling for ½ hour, drain them and arrange them in a baking pan. Cover with the sauce and bake in a hot (400°F.) oven ½ hour, basting frequently.
    Serves 4.

GRILLED KNOCKWURST

1 pound knockwurst

Separate the sausages. Place on broiler grill 4 to 5 inches from the heat and, turning to brown on all sides, cook until browned to your taste. Serve with Bavarian Sauerkraut (see page 131).
    Serves 4.

VEAL FRICASSEE

> 2 pounds boned shoulder of veal
> 1 veal bone
> 1 cup diced celery
> 2 medium onions, coarsely cut
> 6 carrots, cut up
>   Salt and pepper
> 2 tablespoons butter
> 2 tablespoons flour

Have the veal diced in about 1¼-inch squares. Scald the meat in boiling water. Pour off the water and cover the veal with salted water. Add veal bone and boil 30 minutes. Add celery, onion, and carrots. Cook until done (about 15 minutes). Season to taste with salt and pepper. Remove veal bone. Melt the butter, add the flour, and stir until smooth. Add half of the gravy and continue cooking over medium heat, stirring constantly, until thickened. Return the thickened gravy to the pot and stir in well.

Serves 4 to 6.

VEAL SCALLOPINE

> 1½ pounds veal cutlet, cut for scallopine
>   Flour
>   Salt and pepper
> 1 tablespoon butter
> 2 tablespoons olive oil
> ½ cup sliced onion
> ½ cup green pepper strips

2 tablespoons tomato purée
1 cup veal or chicken stock

Dredge the veal with flour and season with salt and pepper. Brown lightly in butter and oil. Add remaining ingredients, cover, and simmer for 20 to 30 minutes.
Serves 4.

CHICKEN A LA KING

2 cups diced cooked chicken
4 tablespoons butter
4 tablespoons flour
1 cup cream
1 cup chicken stock
  Salt and pepper
6 mushrooms, diced
¼ cup diced green pepper
2 pimientos, diced

Melt the butter. Add the flour and blend until smooth. Add cream and chicken stock and cook over medium heat, stirring constantly, until thickened. Season to taste with salt and pepper. Cook the mushrooms and green pepper in water until soft. Drain well. Mix chicken, cooked mushrooms and pepper, pimientos, and sauce. Allow to heat through. Serve on toast, in individual casseroles, or in patty shells.
Serves 4.

TURKEY A LA KING

Follow recipe for Chicken à la King.

VEAL A LA KING

Follow recipe for Chicken à la King.

CREAMED CHICKEN

>   2 cups diced cooked chicken
>   4 tablespoons butter
>   4 tablespoons flour
>   1 cup cream
>   1 cup chicken stock
>   Salt and pepper
>   8 mushrooms, diced and steamed

Melt the butter and add flour, blending until smooth. Add cream and chicken stock and cook over medium heat, stirring constantly, until thickened. Season to taste with salt and pepper. Add chicken and heat thoroughly. Add well-drained mushrooms.

Serves 4.

Note: The reason for steaming the mushrooms, rather than sautéeing them, is that sautéeing makes them very dark and spoils the appearance of the creamed chicken.

CHICKEN CROQUETTES

    2 cups ground chicken
    1 cup thick white sauce
    2 teaspoons chopped parsley
    1 tablespoon powdered chicken stock
      Salt and pepper
      Flour
      Egg Batter (see page 156)
      Bread or corn-flake crumbs
      Sauce Supreme (see page 154)

Mix the chicken, white sauce, parsley, and chicken stock. Season to taste with salt and pepper. Chill the mixture thoroughly. Shape into croquettes, dip in flour, then Egg Batter, then crumbs. Fry in deep fat (375°F.) until nicely browned. Serve with Sauce Supreme.

    Serves 6.

TURKEY CUTLETS

Substitute turkey for the ground chicken in Chicken Croquette recipe. When chilled, shape into cutlets and proceed as for Chicken Croquettes.

BOOKBINDER'S CHICKEN MARYLAND

    1 3-pound broiler, quartered
      Flour
      Salt and pepper
      Egg Batter (see page 156)
      Corn-flake crumbs

Poach chicken pieces in a little water for 15 minutes. Remove from water and dry. Roll chicken in flour, seasoned with salt and pepper; dip the pieces into batter, then roll them in crumbs. Fry in deep fat, 375°F., until nicely browned (10 to 15 minutes).
    Serves 4.

BAKED CHICKEN LOAF

    3 cups ground chicken
    1 cup thick white sauce
    2 eggs
    2 teaspoons chopped parsley
    2 tablespoons chopped green pepper
    1 tablespoon chicken stock
    1 pimiento, chopped
      Salt and pepper to taste
      Brown Chicken Gravy (see page 155)

Mix together thoroughly all ingredients except gravy. Press into meat loaf pan, 9 x 5 x 2½ inches. Bake in a moderate (350°F.) oven ½ hour, or until lightly browned on top. Serve with Brown Chicken Gravy.
    Serves 6.

CHICKEN MEXICAN

    2 cups cooked, diced chicken
    1 cup Creole Sauce (see page 146)
    ½ cup cooked peas
      Dash of Tabasco

To the Creole Sauce, add chicken, peas and Tabasco to taste.
Heat well, and serve on hot dry rice.
    Serves 4.

CHICKEN POT PIE

    2 cups diced cooked chicken
    ½ cup diced celery
    2 medium onions, diced
    2 medium potatoes, diced
    ½ cup shelled peas
    5 tablespoons chicken fat
    4 tablespoons flour
    1 tablespoon powdered chicken stock base
    2½ cups chicken stock
      Salt and pepper
      Flaky pie crust

Cook the vegetables and drain well. Arrange chicken and vegetables in four individual dishes. Melt the chicken fat, add flour,
and stir until smooth. Add powdered chicken stock base and
stock and stir constantly until smooth and thickened. Season to
taste with salt and pepper. Pour gravy over the meat and vegetables and top with pie crust. Seal well at the edges and prick

in the center to allow steam to escape. Bake in a hot (400°F.) oven 25 to 30 minutes, or until crust is nicely browned.

Serves 4.

CREOLE STUFFED PEPPERS

    4 green peppers
    2 tablespoons minced onion
    2 tablespoons minced celery
    1 tablespoon butter
    2 cups chopped cooked chicken
    2 cups cooked rice
    1 egg, beaten
    ½ cup bread crumbs
    ¼ cup milk
       Salt and pepper to taste
    3 cups Creole Sauce (see page 146)

Cut off tops of peppers. Cut the peppers in half lengthwise; remove seeds and membranes. Sauté onion and celery in butter until soft, but not brown. Mix well with all other ingredients except Creole Sauce. Fill the pepper halves with this mixture and place them in a greased baking dish. Pour Creole Sauce over the peppers. Bake in a moderate (350°F.) oven 40 to 45 minutes, or until peppers are done to your taste.

Serves 4 or 8, depending upon appetites.

BRAISED BROILERS

    1 3-pound broiler, cut in half
    3 tablespoons butter

   1 medium onion, sliced
   ¼ cup chopped celery
   1 cup stewed tomatoes
    Salt and pepper

Brown the chicken in the butter. Remove chicken from skillet; cook onion and celery in the same pan until golden brown. Return chicken to skillet, add tomatoes, and season with salt and pepper. Simmer, covered, for 20 to 30 minutes, or until chicken is tender.

    Serves 4.

SOUTHERN FRIED CHICKEN

   1 broiler, quartered
    Salt and pepper
    Paprika
    Flour
   ¼ cup butter

Season the chicken pieces with salt, pepper, and paprika. Dredge with flour. Melt the butter; add chicken pieces and brown them on all sides. Lower the heat, cover the pan, and cook until the chicken is done (about 20 minutes). Serve with Blueberry Fritters (see page 125).

    Serves 4.

TURKEY TETRAZINI

2 cups diced cooked turkey
½ pound spaghetti
½ pound mushrooms
4 tablespoons butter
2 tablespoons flour
1 cup chicken or turkey stock
1 cup cream
2 tablespoons sherry
Salt and pepper
Grated Parmesan cheese

Break up the spaghetti and cook 9 minutes in boiling, salted water. Drain well. Slice the mushrooms with stems and sauté in butter 5 minutes. Sprinkle the flour over the mushrooms and stir to blend well. Add stock and cream and cook over medium heat, stirring constantly, until thickened. Add sherry and season to taste with salt and pepper. Add turkey and heat through. Line a baking dish with the spaghetti and pour the turkey mixture into the center. Sprinkle liberally with grated Parmesan cheese and bake in a hot (400°F.) oven until top is golden (20 to 25 minutes).

Serves 4.

Vegetables
and
Pastas

PICKLED BEETS

    1 bunch beets
    Vinegar and beet stock to cover (half and half)
    1 tablespoon sugar
    1 teaspoon whole allspice
    1 medium onion, sliced

Cut off the tops of the beets, leaving 1 inch of stem. Wash very thoroughly. Cook in boiling, salted water until tender. Skin and slice. Pour over enough beet stock and vinegar, mixed half and half, to cover. Add sugar, allspice, and onion; let stand. If the beets are warm they will be pickled in a half hour, but the longer you leave them in the marinade, the better. Serve cold.

CORN FRITTERS

    2 cups flour
    3 teaspoons baking powder
    ½ teaspoon salt
    3 egg yolks, well beaten
    1½ cups milk
    ¼ cup melted butter
    3 egg whites, beaten stiff
    2 cups uncooked corn kernels

Mix and sift dry ingredients. Add egg yolks to milk and mix well. Add melted butter and mix again. Add to dry ingredients and beat until smooth. Fold in stiffly beaten egg whites. Add corn, newly sliced off the cob, and mix well. Drop by spoonfuls onto hot griddle and fry, turning once to brown both sides lightly.

Serves 6.

BLUEBERRY FRITTERS

Substitute 2 cups of blueberries for the corn in Corn Fritter recipe.

APPLE FRITTERS

Substitute 2 cups apple slices for corn in Corn Fritter recipe.

PEPPER CORN

    4 large ears corn
    4 tablespoons butter
   ¼ cup milk or light cream
   ½ cup chopped green pepper
    2 pimientos, chopped
      Salt and pepper

Cut the kernels from the ears of corn and cook them gently, over low heat, in the butter and milk or cream for about 5 minutes. Add green pepper and pimientos and allow to heat through, adding a tiny bit more milk or cream, if necessary. Season to taste with salt and pepper.

Serves 4.

CORN MEXICAN

4 large ears corn
1 cup Creole Sauce (page 146)
Tabasco to taste

Cut the kernels from the ears of corn and cook them 5 minutes in the Creole Sauce with Tabasco added to make it as hot as you like.

Serves 4.

FRENCH-FRIED EGGPLANT

1 large eggplant
Flour, seasoned with salt and pepper
Egg Batter (see page 156)
Corn-flake crumbs

Peel eggplant and cut into fingers, about the same size as French-fried potatoes. Roll the pieces in seasoned flour, dip in Egg Batter, and roll in crumbs. Fry in deep fat (375°F.) until nicely browned (about 8 minutes).

Serves 4 to 6.

MACARONI AND CHEESE

½ pound elbow macaroni
2 cups medium white sauce
½ pound Cheddar cheese, grated
Paprika
Butter

Cook the macaroni in boiling, salted water 9 minutes. Drain well. Mix with the cream sauce and half the grated cheese. Place in a baking dish, cover with the remaining cheese, and sprinkle paprika over all. Dot with butter and bake in a hot (400°F.) oven until nicely browned (20 to 30 minutes).

Serves 4.

SPANISH MACARONI

½ pound elbow macaroni
2 cups Creole Sauce (see page 146)
½ cup grated sharp Cheddar cheese
½ cup bread crumbs
    Butter

Cook the macaroni in boiling, salted water 9 minutes. Drain well and place in a baking dish. Add Creole Sauce and mix well. Cover with cheese and bread crumbs, mixed, and dot well with butter. Bake in a hot (400°F.) oven until top is nicely browned (20 to 30 minutes).

Serves 4.

FRENCH-FRIED ONIONS

4 Bermuda onions
    Flour, seasoned with salt, pepper, and paprika
    Egg Batter (see page 156)
    Cracker meal

Peel onions, cutting off both ends. Cut into ½-inch slices and separate into rings. Dip into seasoned flour, then into batter, then

into cracker meal. Fry in deep fat (375°F.) until golden brown.
Serves 4 to 6.

BROWNED TINY PEARL ONIONS

    1 1-pound can pearl onions
      Salt and pepper
      Paprika
    1 tablespoon sugar
      Butter

Drain onions well and place in a baking pan. Sprinkle with salt,
pepper, paprika, and sugar. Dot generously with butter. Bake in
a very hot (450°F.) oven, turning occasionally, until browned
(12 to 15 minutes).
Serves 4.

FRENCH-FRIED POTATOES

    4 large potatoes
      Salt and pepper

Peel potatoes and cut them into strips about ½-inch thick. Soak
in cold water to cover for ½ hour. Dry thoroughly with absorbent
paper. Fry in deep fat (375°F.) for 5 minutes. Drain, cool, and
refrigerate. Just before serving, fry in deep fat (400° F., or higher
if your fryer permits) until brown and crisp.
Serves 4.

HASHED BROWN POTATOES

    2 cups cubed cooked potatoes
      Salt and pepper
    2 tablespoons butter
    2 tablespoons vegetable oil
      Paprika

Season the potato cubes with salt and pepper. Melt butter with oil in a skillet. Add potatoes and press them down firmly. Cover and cook over low heat until golden brown (20 to 30 minutes). Sprinkle with paprika and turn carefully with a spatula to brown the other side.

    Serves 4.

LYONNAISE POTATOES

    4 large boiled potatoes
    2 tablespoons butter
    2 tablespoons vegetable oil
      Salt and pepper
    2 medium onions, sliced thin

Peel the potatoes and slice them in medium-thick slices. Melt the butter with the oil in a skillet. Place a layer of half the potatoes in this and season with salt and pepper. Cover with the onion slices and season them. Cover with the rest of the potato slices and season again. Cook, covered, over low heat until brown on the bottom (20 to 30 minutes). Turn carefully with a spatula and brown the other side.

    Serves 4.

O'BRIEN POTATOES

2 cups diced cooked potatoes
2 tablespoons diced green pepper
2 pimientos, diced
2 tablespoons butter
2 tablespoons vegetable oil

Mix potatoes, green pepper, and pimiento. Melt butter with oil in a skillet. Add potato mixture and press down firmly. Cover and cook over low heat until golden brown. Turn upside down to serve.
Serves 4.

SPANISH BROWN POTATOES

8 small potatoes
Salt and pepper
Paprika
Butter

Try to have the potatoes as nearly the same size as possible. Peel the potatoes and place them in a baking pan. Sprinkle with salt, pepper, and paprika; dot with butter. Bake in a slow (325°F.) oven until brown (30 to 45 minutes).
Serves 4.

CANDIED SWEET POTATOES

  1 cup sugar
½ cup water
½ cup orange juice
  2 tablespoons lemon juice
½ lemon, cut in slices
½ orange, cut in slices
  4 large cooked sweet potatoes

Combine all ingredients except potatoes. Simmer for about 30 minutes. Cut potatoes in quarters, or slices if you prefer, and place in a baking dish. Strain the syrup over them and bake in a hot (400°F.) oven for 10 minutes.

    Serves 4.

BAVARIAN SAUERKRAUT

  1 1-pound can sauerkraut
  4 slices bacon
  1 cup canned tomatoes, drained
  1 apple
  1 tablespoon minced onion
½ teaspoon salt
  1 tablespoon sugar

Drain the sauerkraut well. (If you buy fresh kraut from the butcher, drain well, cover with boiling water and cook half an hour. Drain well again.) Partially cook the bacon slices; cut each slice in four pieces. Wash, peel, and core the apple and cut it into eight pieces. Place all ingredients in a saucepan and heat gently until tender (15 to 20 minutes), adding a very little water, if necessary.

Serves 4.

SCALLOPED TOMATOES

        3 cups stewed tomatoes
        1 cup soft bread crumbs
        2 tablespoons minced onions
        ¾ cup grated Cheddar cheese
        1 tablespoon sugar
        1 teaspoon salt
           Dash of freshly ground pepper
        ¼ cup dry bread crumbs
           Butter for dotting

Mix tomatoes with soft bread crumbs, onions, ½ cup Cheddar cheese, sugar, salt, and pepper. Place the mixture in a baking dish. Mix the remaining ¼ cup grated Cheddar with the dry bread crumbs and sprinkle over the dish. Dot with butter. Bake in a hot (400°F.) oven 20 minutes, or until nicely browned.

Serves 4 to 6.

SAUTEED ZUCCHINI

        2 medium zucchini
        2 tablespoons butter
        1 small onion, sliced
        1 teaspoon powdered chicken stock
           Salt and pepper

Slice the zucchini in ½-inch slices. Melt the butter in a skillet. Add zucchini, onion and powdered stock, and sauté until the zucchini is soft (about 10 minutes), but not brown, adding more butter if necessary. Season to taste with salt and pepper.

Serves 4.

Salads

CHICKEN SALAD WITH FRIED OYSTERS

        2 cups diced cooked chicken
        ½ cup diced celery
        1 teaspoon celery salt
        1 teaspoon paprika
          Salt and pepper to taste
        ½ cup mayonnaise (or more, to taste)
          Lettuce leaves
        16 fried oysters (see page 67)

Mix chicken and celery with seasonings and mayonnaise. Place
each serving on a lettuce leaf and keep well chilled until oysters
are piping hot and brown. Serve at once.
    Serves 4.

COLE SLAW

        1 medium head cabbage, shredded
        ½ green pepper, shredded
        3 tablespoons sugar
        1 teaspoon salt
        3 tablespoons vinegar
        1 small carrot, grated

  1 cup mayonnaise, or to taste
  Celery seed

Mix together all ingredients except celery seed. Be sure to blend thoroughly. Marinate overnight in refrigerator. Sprinkle with celery seed before serving.
  Serves 4.

SPRING SALAD

Follow the preceding recipe for Cole Slaw, but use about ½ cup olive oil in place of the mayonnaise.

CUCUMBER SALAD

  2 large cucumbers
  1 medium onion
  ½ cup vinegar
  2 tablespoons sugar
  ¼ cup water

Peel cucumbers and score them. Slice them into ice water in not-too-thin slices. Drain and pat dry. Peel onion, slice thinly, and add to cucumber slices. Pour vinegar, sugar, and water over the slices, adding more water if necessary. Refrigerate overnight, if possible—or in any event, several hours. Serve as a side dish on lettuce or not, as you please.
  Serves 4.

TOSSED GREEN SALAD

At Bookbinder's this is a combination of escarole, endive, fine-cut celery, shredded carrots, sliced tomato and lettuce. The dressing used is "1890," which comes in a bottle and is excellent.

MACARONI SALAD

        8 ounces elbow macaroni
        2 tablespoons diced green pepper
        2 tablespoons diced celery
        2 pimientos, diced
        ½ teaspoon salt
           White pepper to taste
        ½ teaspoon celery salt
        1 cup mayonnaise (or to taste)

Cook the macaroni in boiling, salted water 9 minutes. Drain well. Cool and chill. Mix with other ingredients and let stand in refrigerator overnight.
    Serves 4.

LOBSTER SALAD

        1 cup cooked lobster, cubed
        ⅓ cup chopped celery
        ¼ cup mayonnaise (or to taste)

Mix all ingredients together and chill thoroughly. Serve on beds of lettuce.
    Serves 2.

Note: This is the way Bookbinder's serves all seafood salads—shrimp, crabmeat, or combinations of two or more.

SALMON SALAD

    2 cups cooked salmon
    1 cup diced celery
      Salt
      White pepper
    ½ cup mayonnaise (or to taste)

Flake the salmon and mix with the celery. Season to taste with salt and pepper and mix with mayonnaise. Serve, well chilled, on lettuce.
    Serves 4.

Note: Bookbinder's makes halibut salad and tuna fish salad in the same way.

SARDINE SALAD

    1 head Boston lettuce
    2 tomatoes, cut in eighths
    1 small cucumber, sliced
    8 radishes, thinly sliced
    ½ green pepper, cut in strips
    3 scallions, sliced
    1 bunch water cress
    1 tin boneless and skinless sardines
    1 hard-cooked egg, sliced
    ½ cup French dressing

Line a salad bowl with lettuce. Mix the tomatoes, cucumber, radishes, green pepper strips, scallions, and water cress and place in the center of the bowl. Top with sardines and decorate with egg slices. When ready to serve, pour dressing over the salad and mix gently.

Serves 4 to 6.

TOMATOES STUFFED WITH CRABMEAT

        6 large ripe tomatoes
        1 cup lump crabmeat
        ½ cup chopped celery
        ½ teaspoon salt
          White pepper to taste
        ¼ cup mayonnaise (or to taste)
        1 hard-cooked egg, chopped
        1 tablespoon minced parsley
          Paprika
          Ripe olives
          Green olives

Hollow out the tomatoes, removing the stem end. Mix crabmeat and celery with salt, white pepper, and mayonnaise. Stuff the tomatoes with the mixture. Sprinkle with chopped egg and top each with a little parsley and a dash of paprika. Serve with ripe and green olives on the side.

Serves 6.

FRUIT SALAD

> Fruit
> Lettuce
> Cottage cheese

This is served at Bookbinder's with a mixture of four varieties of fruit, cut up (whatever is in season which goes well with the rest). The fruit is placed on lettuce and topped with cottage cheese. It is usually served without dressing. Fruits good to use in such a salad are: apples, melons, strawberries, raspberries, blueberries, oranges, grapefruit, pineapple, grapes, pears, or any other kind which suits your fancy.

HONEYDEW BOAT

> 1 honeydew melon
> 1 cup diced fresh fruits
> 4 tablespoons cottage cheese

Cut melon in half and remove seeds. Remove meat of melon with a ball cutter and mix with other diced fresh fruit. Return to melon halves and place 2 tablespoons cottage cheese on top of each.
　　Serves 2.

Sauces
and
Dressings

SAUCE AMANDINE

½ cup butter
½ teaspoon Worcestershire sauce
½ cup blanched almonds, slivered
2 tablespoons minced parsley

Melt the butter. Add Worcestershire sauce and almonds; cook to brown the nuts delicately. Add parsley and pour over fish or seafood.

ANCHOVY SAUCE

1 can flat anchovy fillets
¼ pound butter
1 tablespoon lemon juice
1 tablespoon minced parsley

Drain the anchovy fillets well and chop. Melt the butter. Add fillets, lemon juice, and parsley, and heat until sizzling, but do not let the butter brown.

BECHAMEL SAUCE

> 2 tablespoons butter
> 2 tablespoons flour
> 1 tablespoon finely chopped onion
> 1 cup chicken broth
> 2 tablespoons heavy cream
>   Salt and pepper

Melt the butter. Add flour and stir until smooth. Stir in chopped onion. Add chicken broth slowly, stirring constantly until thickened. Add cream, season to taste with salt and pepper, and simmer very gently for about 15 minutes. Strain.

Makes about 1 cup sauce.

BORDELAISE SAUCE

> 2 tablespoons butter
> 2 tablespoons flour
> 2 cups stock (can be made from a bouillon cube)
> 3 cloves garlic, minced
> 2 tablespoons chopped onion
> 1 bay leaf
> 1 tablespoon Worcestershire sauce
> 1 tablespoon chili sauce
>   Salt and pepper
> 2 tablespoons sherry

Melt the butter in a sauce pan. Add flour; stir to blend. Cook until brown. Gradually add stock, garlic, onion, bay leaf, Worcestershire and chili sauce. Cook, stirring constantly, until thickened and well blended, about 5 minutes. Strain sauce and season with salt and pepper. Add sherry.

Makes about 2 cups sauce.

COCKTAIL SAUCE

>   1 cup tomato catsup
>   Freshly grated horseradish to taste
>   1 teaspoon Worcestershire sauce

Mix all ingredients together. It is probably best to go light on the horseradish and to serve a little dish of it for those who wish to make their sauce hotter. If you can't find fresh horseradish root, use the bottled or dehydrated type, of course.

CREOLE SAUCE

>   2 tablespoons chopped green pepper
>   2 tablespoons chopped onion
>   2 tablespoons chopped celery
>   1 clove garlic, mashed
>   4 tablespoons butter
>   1 large can tomatoes
>   1 teaspoon Worcestershire
>   1 bay leaf
>   ½ cup chicken stock
>   1 veal bone
>   Salt and pepper to taste
>   Few drops of Tabasco (optional)

Sauté green pepper, onion, celery, and garlic in butter over low heat about 10 minutes. Add remaining ingredients and simmer, covered, 45 minutes. Remove veal bone and bay leaf and correct seasoning.

Makes about 2 cups sauce.

EGG SAUCE

>   4 tablespoons butter
>   4 tablespoons flour
>   2 cups scalded milk
>   Salt and pepper
>   2 hard-cooked eggs

Melt the butter. Blend in flour, stirring until smooth. Add scalded milk slowly, and cook, stirring constantly, until thickened. Season to taste with salt and pepper. Chop eggs coarsely and add. Heat through.

Makes about 2¼ cups sauce.

GARLIC BUTTER SAUCE

>   ¼ pound (1 stick) butter
>   2 cloves garlic, mashed

Melt the butter, but do not allow it to brown. Add the garlic and simmer gently to let the butter absorb the flavor of the garlic.

Makes about ½ cup sauce.

HORSERADISH SAUCE

>   2 tablespoons butter
>   2 tablespoons flour
>   1 cup beef stock
>   Horseradish

Melt the butter and blend in flour, stirring until smooth. Add stock and cook, stirring constantly, until thickened. Add horse-radish to taste. Serve hot.

Makes about 1 cup sauce.

LAMAZE SAUCE

>   1 cup mayonnaise
>   1 cup chili sauce
>   1 cup India relish, *well drained*
>   1 teaspoon prepared mustard
>   1 teaspoon Worcestershire sauce
>   1 tablespoon horseradish
>   1 drop Tabasco
>   1 hard-cooked egg, chopped
>   Good grind of black pepper
>   1 pimiento, chopped
>   1 tablespoon chopped chives
>   1 teaspoon Escoffier Sauce Diable

Mix all ingredients together thoroughly. Refrigerate until needed.

Makes about 3 cups sauce.

LEMON BUTTER SAUCE

    ¼ pound (1 stick) butter
    2 tablespoons lemon juice

Melt the butter, but do not allow it to brown. Add lemon juice
and heat gently.

Makes about ½ cup of lemon butter.

LOBSTER SAUCE

    3 tablespoons butter
    3 tablespoons flour
    1 teaspoon salt
      Dash of freshly ground pepper
    1 cup milk
    ½ cup cream
    ¼ cup dry sherry
    1 to 1½ cups cooked, diced lobster

Melt the butter. Add the flour, salt, and pepper; stir to blend
smoothly. Continue cooking over medium heat. Pour milk and
cream in gradually, stirring constantly until the sauce thickens.
Reduce heat and cook gently for 2 minutes. Add sherry and lobster and let cook just long enough to heat through.

Makes about 3 cups sauce.

Note: If Lobster Sauce must be reheated it should be done in a
double boiler over hot water, *not* over direct heat.

MUSHROOM SAUCE

½ pound mushrooms
2 tablespoons butter
2 tablespoons flour
1 cup thin cream
  Salt and pepper

Peel the mushrooms, if necessary. Slice thin, including the stems. Sauté in butter 5 minutes. Sprinkle with flour and stir gently to mix well. Add cream and stir until thickened. Season to taste with salt and pepper.

Makes about 1½ cups sauce.

NEWBURG SAUCE

1 tablespoon butter
1 teaspoon flour
1 cup cream
2 egg yolks
2 tablespoons sherry
1 tablespoon brandy
  Salt and pepper
  Dash of cayenne pepper

Melt the butter. Add the flour and stir until smooth. Add cream and stir to blend well. Beat egg yolks with the sherry and add. Add brandy, stir well, and season to taste with salt, pepper, and cayenne. *Do not allow sauce to boil.*

Makes about 1¼ cups sauce.

OYSTER SAUCE I

¼ cup oyster liquor
½ cup cream
1 egg yolk
   Salt and pepper
1 tablespoon lemon juice

Heat the oyster liquor and cream together. Beat the egg yolk, add a little of the heated cream mixture, and beat well. Return to the remaining cream and beat in briskly. Season to taste with salt and pepper and beat in the lemon juice.

Makes about ¾ cup sauce.

OYSTER SAUCE II

3 tablespoons butter
2 tablespoons flour
¼ teaspoon salt
   Dash of freshly ground pepper
1 cup hot cream
1 dozen oysters, chopped
   Oyster liquor to taste
1 teaspoon lemon juice
1 tablespoon minced parsley

Melt the butter. Add flour, salt, and pepper; stir until smooth. Add cream and stir constantly until the sauce thickens. The easiest way to chop oysters is to put them into the blender with a little of their liquor and turn it on and almost immediately off. Add the chopped oysters to the sauce and as much of their liquor as you like. Stir in lemon juice and parsley.

Makes 1½ to 2 cups sauce.

ᴘARSLEY BUTTER SAUCE

    ¼ pound (1 stick) butter
    2 tablespoons finely minced parsley

Cream the butter and parsley together and refrigerate until ready to use. Place, cold, to melt on the food for which it is desired.

SHRIMP NEWBURG SAUCE

    1 tablespoon butter
    1 teaspoon flour
    1 cup heavy cream
       Salt and pepper
       Cayenne pepper
    ½ cup chopped, cooked shrimp
    2 egg yolks
    3 tablespoons sherry

Melt the butter. Stir in flour and blend until smooth. Add cream and stir until hot and well blended. Add salt and pepper to taste and a few grains of cayenne pepper. Add shrimp and heat, but do not boil. Add a little of the sauce to the egg yolks and beat well. Add to the sauce, together with the sherry. Stir well and heat, but *do not boil.*

LOBSTER NEWBURG SAUCE

Follow the preceding recipe for Shrimp Newburg Sauce, but substitute chopped lobster for the shrimp.

TARTARE SAUCE

    1 cup mayonnaise
    1 tablespoon minced onion
    1 tablespoon minced parsley
    1 tablespoon chopped olives (optional)
    2 tablespoons green pickle relish, *well drained*

Mix all ingredients together well and refrigerate for several hours before serving.

Makes about 1 cup sauce.

TOMATO SAUCE

    3 tablespoons butter
    1 stalk celery, chopped fine
    1 medium onion, chopped
    1 tablespoon chopped parsley
    1 clove garlic, mashed
    1 large can tomatoes
    1 tablespoon tomato paste
    1 teaspoon salt
      Freshly ground pepper
    1 teaspoon dried basil
    1 bay leaf

Melt the butter. Add celery, onion, parsley, and garlic; sauté until browned. Add tomatoes and tomato paste. Season with salt and pepper. Simmer gently for 45 minutes. Add basil and bay leaf and simmer 15 minutes longer. Remove bay leaf and whirl the sauce in the blender or press it through a sieve.

Makes about 1½ to 2 cups sauce.

SAUCE SUPREME

2 tablespoons butter
2 tablespoons flour
½ cup mushroom liquor
½ cup chicken stock
2 tablespoons heavy cream
1 egg yolk
Salt to taste

Melt butter, stir in flour, and cook briefly; do not brown. Add mushroom liquor, stock, and cream; stir until thickened. With a wire whisk, beat in egg yolk. Season to taste with salt.

FISH STOCK

Every time you cook fish in water, save the resultant stock and cook it down a bit to strengthen it. Freeze for use when needed.

You can also make fish stock when needed, thus.

Fish bones and head
2 cups dry white wine
1 tablespoon minced onion
Pinch of thyme
1 bay leaf

Sprig of parsley
Salt and pepper

Cook all together at a simmer for 30 to 45 minutes. Strain through several thicknesses of cheesecloth.

Makes about 1¼ cups stock.

PLAIN STUFFING FOR FISH

1 cup bread crumbs
½ cup hot water
½ cup melted butter
¼ teaspoon salt
1 tablespoon minced onion
½ teaspoon thyme
   Freshly ground pepper

Mix all together lightly with a fork.

Makes 1 cup of stuffing.

BROWN CHICKEN GRAVY

2 tablespoons butter
2 tablespoons flour
1 cup chicken stock
1 tablespoon powdered chicken stock

Melt the butter. Stir in flour and continue stirring until the mixture is smooth and the flour has browned. Be careful not to let it burn. Add stock and powdered stock and stir constantly until thickened. Correct seasoning.

Makes 1 cup gravy.

EGG BATTER

>   1 cup milk
>   1 egg
>   ½ teaspoon salt

Beat all ingredients together thoroughly.

BLUE CHEESE DRESSING

>   3 tablespoons olive oil
>   1 tablespoon mild vinegar
>   1 tablespoon crumbled Blue cheese

Mix all ingredients together well.
  This makes enough dressing to use on a green salad for 4.

SOUR CREAM–ROQUEFORT DRESSING

>   ¼ cup sour cream
>   1 tablespoon crumbled Roquefort cheese
>   Salt to taste
>   Milk

Mix sour cream, Roquefort cheese, and salt. Thin to taste with milk.
  This makes enough dressing to use on a green salad for 4.

Sandwiches

CHEESE DELIGHT

>   3 thin slices Cheddar cheese
>   2 slices bread
>   Egg Batter (see page 156)
>   Cracker crumbs

Put the cheese slices between the bread slices. Dip in Egg Batter, then in cracker crumbs. Fry in deep fat (375°F.) until nicely brown.
    Serves 1.

Note: A slice of ham may be substituted for one of the cheese slices. *Or,* substitute 2 slices of cooked bacon for one of the cheese slices.

GRILLED CHEESE SANDWICH

>   1 fairly thick slice Cheddar cheese
>   1 slice toast

Put the cheese on the toast and broil until cheese is slightly brown.
    Serves 1.

GRILLED BACON AND CHEESE SANDWICH

    1 fairly thick slice Cheddar cheese
    1 slice toast
    2 slices bacon, partially cooked

Put the cheese on the toast and place bacon slices on top. Broil until bacon is crisp.

    Serves 1.

CHICKEN SALAD SANDWICH

    1 cup finely diced cooked chicken
    2 tablespoons finely chopped celery
    1 tablespoon finely chopped green pepper
    1 tablespoon finely chopped pimiento
    2 to 3 tablespoons mayonnaise
      Salt and white pepper to taste
      Celery salt to taste

Mix all ingredients together thoroughly. Serve on toast or buttered rolls.

    Makes 4 sandwiches.

CLUB SANDWICH

    3 slices white toast
      Butter
    1 lettuce leaf
    1 or 2 slices chicken
      Salt and pepper
      Mayonnaise
    3 slices tomato
    2 slices cooked bacon

Butter one toast slice. Place the lettuce leaf on it, and top with the chicken. Season to taste with salt and pepper. Spread with mayonnaise. Butter second slice of toast and place it, buttered side up, on top of the chicken. Arrange tomato slices on this piece of toast, add mayonnaise, and top with bacon. Cover with third slice of toast. Cut into four triangles and serve at once.

    Serves 1.

WESTERN CLUB SANDWICH

    3 slices toast
      Butter
    1 slice fried ham
    2 slices American cheese
    3 strips cooked bacon
    1 lettuce leaf
      Tomato
      Dill pickle
      Mayonnaise

Butter the toast. Place the ham and 1 slice of cheese on one of the buttered toast slices. Put under broiler to brown the cheese slightly. Place the second slice of toast over the cheese and arrange the bacon and second slice of cheese on top. Put this under the broiler to brown the cheese. Remove from broiler, top with the lettuce leaf and the last slice of toast. Place the sandwich on a serving plate and cut it in triangles. Serve with sliced tomato and sliced dill pickle. You may also serve a side dish of mayonnaise for those who wish dressing.

Makes 1 sandwich.

LUMP CRAB SANDWICH

    1 cup lump crabmeat
    2 tablespoons finely chopped celery
    1 tablespoon finely chopped green pepper
    1 tablespoon finely chopped pimiento
    2 to 3 tablespoons mayonnaise
      Salt and white pepper
      Celery salt to taste

Pick over the crabmeat carefully to remove all bony fibers. Mix with other ingredients, thoroughly but gently, so as not to break up the crabmeat too much. Serve on toast, buttered roll, or any kind of bread you wish.

Serves 4.

DELMONICO STEAK SANDWICH

    2 green peppers, cut in ½-inch strips
    3 tomatoes, cut in wedges
      Olive oil
    4 cooked minute steaks
   12 slices toast
      Bordelaise Sauce (see page 145)

Cook green peppers and tomatoes in a small amount of olive oil
until soft. Place each cooked steak on two slices of toast which
have been cut into ½-inch strips. Place green pepper and tomatoes alternately over the top of steaks. Spoon Bordelaise sauce over
all. Cut remaining toast in ½-inch strips and serve along with
sandwich.
    Serves 4.

"HAM AND" SANDWICH

    2 slices whole wheat or rye bread
    1 slice baked Virginia ham
    1 small tomato, sliced
    1 lettuce leaf
    4 slices crisp bacon
      Cinnamon apple
      Lamaze Sauce

Butter the bread. On one slice arrange ham, tomato slices, lettuce,
and bacon. Cover with remaining slice of bread. Place the sandwich on a serving plate, cut it once diagonally, and skewer with

toothpicks. Serve with wedges of cinnamon apple and Lamaze
Sauce (page 148).

Makes 1 sandwich.

GRILLED HAM AND CHEESE SANDWICH

1 slice boiled ham
1 slice toast
1 fairly thick slice Cheddar cheese

Place the ham on the toast. Cover with cheese and broil until
cheese is slightly brown.

Serves 1.

FLORIDA HAM SANDWICH

3 ounces cream cheese, softened
1 teaspoon sugar
½ teaspoon grated orange rind
1 tablespoon frozen orange juice concentrate
8 large slices pumpernickel bread
4 slices baked ham (8 ounces)
  Butter or margarine
  Small cold beets
  Lettuce or water cress

Combine softened cream cheese, sugar, and orange rind. Gradually blend in orange juice concentrate until the mixture is smooth
and of spreading consistency. Spread four slices of the bread with
the cream cheese mixture and top each with a slice of ham. Spread
the remaining 4 slices of bread with butter or margarine and

place over ham to close sandwich. Cut diagonally into halves. Serve with small cold beets on lettuce or water cress.

Makes 4 sandwiches.

SARDINE SANDWICH

    1 slice toast
      Butter
    1 lettuce leaf
    3 boneless and skinless sardines
      Mayonnaise, or other preferred spread

Butter the toast. Put lettuce leaf on the toast and arrange the sardines neatly on the lettuce. Serve mayonnaise, Lamaze Sauce (see page 148), or other spread on the side.

Serves 1.

SARDINE AND TOMATO SANDWICH

    1 slice rye toast
      Butter
    3 thin slices tomato
    3 boneless and skinless sardines
      Mayonnaise, or other preferred spread

Butter the toast. Place the tomato slices on the toast and arrange the sardines neatly on top. Serve with mayonnaise or other preferred spread.

Serves 1.

TARGET SANDWICH

  2 slices white bread
    Butter
  2 slices ham
  1 slice American cheese
  1 lettuce leaf
    Mayonnaise, if desired
    Onion slice
    Stuffed olives
    Chopped pickle

Butter the bread. On one piece of bread, place 1 ham slice, the slice of cheese, the remaining ham slice, and the lettuce leaf. Cover with second slice of bread. Place the sandwich on a serving plate and cut it in half. Serve mayonnaise on the side for those who wish it. Serve sandwich with onion slice, stuffed olives, and chopped pickle.

Makes 1 sandwich.

TRAVELERS' DELIGHT

  ½ pound boiled ham
  ½ pound cooked turkey (or chicken)
  1 stalk celery
  ½ green pepper
  1 pimiento
  1 medium-sized dill pickle
  2 hard-cooked eggs
    Salt and pepper to taste
    Mayonnaise
    Potato chips

Grind together the ham, turkey or chicken, celery, green pepper, pimiento, dill pickle, and hard-cooked eggs. Season with salt and pepper and add enough mayonnaise to hold mixture together. Spread on white bread, toast, or rolls. Serve with potato chips.

Makes about 2½ cups, enough for 6 to 8 sandwiches.

Desserts

CHEESE CAKE

Bookbinder's will not divulge its cheese cake recipe, so I have worked out this one, which is the *type* they serve, but not the same. However, I think it's very good, and I hope you will, too!

> Butter for greasing
> Graham cracker crumbs
> 12 ounces cream cheese
> ¾ cup sugar
> 4 egg yolks
> 2 tablespoons flour
> 1½ teaspoons vanilla
> ½ teaspoon salt
> 2 cups scalded light cream
> 4 egg whites, beaten stiff

Grease an 8-inch spring cake form *thickly* with butter. Turn the form on its side, put in a few crumbs and shake them so that they stick to the sides. Keep turning the form and adding more crumbs as necessary. When the sides are well coated, shake a light coating of crumbs onto the bottom. Store in the freezer for at least a half hour, or refrigerate for a couple of hours. Put the cream cheese, sugar, egg yolks, flour, vanilla and salt into a big bowl. Cream until smooth (this is easiest with an electric beater). Add scalded light cream and mix well. Fold in beaten egg whites.

Turn the cheese mixture into the crumbed spring form. Place in a pan with a little hot water in it and bake in a slow (300°F.) oven 1½ hours. Cool. Refrigerate for at least 6 hours before serving.

Makes one 8-inch cheese cake.

Note: This cake has practically no crust, like Bookbinder's. It is also good with a regular graham cracker crust, made according to directions on the crumb package. If you cannot buy the crumbs they are easy to make in the blender from graham crackers.

DEEP-DISH APPLE PIE

    5 to 7 tart apples
    1 quart cold water
    1 tablespoon salt
    1 cup sugar (or to taste)
    ½ teaspoon cinnamon
      Pastry for 6 individual deep dishes or 1 9-inch deep dish
    2 teaspoons butter

Peel, core, and slice the apples into a bowl containing the water and salt. Let the apples stand in the water for 5 minutes, then drain. Mix the sugar and cinnamon and sprinkle over the apples. Blend thoroughly so that the sugar is spread evenly over all the apples. Cover and let stand 15 minutes. Drain, reserving sugar syrup. Fill pastry-lined baking dishes with apple slices and cover with top crust. Make slits in top crust to allow steam to escape Bake in a hot (400°F.) oven 45 to 50 minutes. While pies are baking, add enough water to the reserved sugar syrup to make 1 cup. Bring to boiling, réduce heat, and simmer for 5 minutes; add butter. When pies are baked and cooling pour a little of the

cooked syrup into each pie through the slits in the top crust. Pies
can be served with ice cream, if desired.

Serves 6.

BLUEBERRY PIE

> 1 1-pound can or 2 packages frozen, sweetened blueberries
> (thawed), drained
> ½ cup blueberry juice
> 1 tablespoon cornstarch
> Dash salt
> 1 baked 8-inch pie shell

Drain the blueberries, reserving ½ cup of juice. Mix juice, cornstarch, and salt. Cook over medium heat, stirring constantly, until
clear and thickened. Remove from heat and add drained blueberries. Pour mixture into pie shell. Chill thoroughly before serving.

Makes one 8-inch pie.

CHERRY PIE

> 1 1-pound can pitted sour cherries, drained
> ½ cup cherry juice
> 2½ tablespoons cornstarch
> ¾ cup sugar (or more, to taste)
> Dash salt
> Red food coloring, if desired
> 1 baked 8-inch pie shell

Drain the cherries, reserving ½ cup of the juice. Mix cherry juice,
cornstarch, sugar, and salt. Cook over medium heat, stirring con-

stantly, until clear and thickened. Remove from heat; add a drop
of red food coloring to intensify color, if desired. Add drained
cherries, blend thoroughly, and pour into the baked pie shell.
Chill well before serving.

Makes one 8-inch pie.

FRESH COCONUT-CUSTARD PIE

      4 eggs, well beaten
    ½ cup sugar
    ¼ teaspoon salt
      2 cups hot milk
    ½ teaspoon vanilla
      1 cup freshly grated coconut
      1 9-inch unbaked pie shell

Combine the beaten eggs, sugar, and salt; add milk very gradually, stirring constantly so that the custard does not curdle. Stir
in the vanilla. Spread the coconut over the bottom of the un-
baked pie shell and pour custard mixture over it. Bake in a hot
(450°F.) oven 10 minutes; then reduce heat to 350°F. and bake
25 to 30 minutes longer, or until a knife inserted in the custard
comes out clean.

Makes one 9-inch pie.

LEMON CREAM PIE

¾ cup water
1¾ cups sugar (or to taste)
¼ teaspoon salt
3 eggs, separated
½ cup lemon juice
6 tablespoons cornstarch
5 tablespoons butter
1 partially baked 10-inch pie shell

Mix the water, sugar, and salt in the top of a double boiler over hot, not boiling, water. Bring to a boil. Beat egg yolks and lemon juice, add cornstarch, and blend thoroughly. Gradually add to the sugar syrup in the top of the double boiler. Cook, stirring constantly, for 10 minutes. Add butter and fold in stiffly beaten egg whites. Pour into partially baked pie shell. Bake in a moderate (350°F.) oven for 15 minutes or until top is golden brown. Allow to cool; chill thoroughly before serving. You may serve this pie with whipped cream.

LEMON SPONGE PIE

1 tablespoon butter
1 cup sugar
2 egg yolks
Rind of 1 lemon
Juice of 1 lemon
2 tablespoons flour
1 cup milk

2 egg whites, stiffly beaten
1 partially baked 10-inch pie shell

Cream the butter and gradually add the sugar; beat until well blended. Add, one at a time, the egg yolks, rind and juice of lemon, flour, and milk. Blend thoroughly after each addition. Fold in stiffly beaten egg whites. Pour into partially baked pie shell. Bake in a moderate (350°F.) oven for 15 minutes or until top becomes golden brown.

Makes one 10-inch pie.

CREAM PUFF SHELLS

¼ cup water
1 cup heavy cream
⅛ teaspoon salt
¾ cup flour
5 eggs

Place water, cream, and salt in a heavy saucepan and heat; when boiling briskly, add flour all at once, stirring vigorously with a wooden spoon. Beat until the mixture forms a smooth ball. Cool slightly. Add the eggs one at a time, beating thoroughly after each addition. Continue beating until the mixture is thick, smooth, and glossy, and breaks off when the spoon is raised. With a spoon, mound the dough on a greased baking sheet, putting mounds 2 inches apart to allow for spreading. Bake in a hot (450°F.) oven for 15 minutes, then reduce heat to 350°F. and bake 20 to 25 minutes longer. Remove from baking sheet and cool. Fill with desired filling.

Makes about 12 large puffs.

PUFF PASTE

>   1 cup (2 sticks) butter
> 1½ cups flour
>   ½ teaspoon salt
>   ½ cup ice water

Remove the butter from the refrigerator. Sift the flour and salt together. Stir in ice water with a fork, then knead the dough until it is smooth. On a floured board, roll the dough into a neat rectangle, about 6 inches wide by 11 inches long. Slice sticks of butter three times lengthwise and place the slices on the upper half of the rectangle of dough, laying them across the width and leaving a ½-inch margin. Fold the lower half of the dough up over the butter and press the edges together. Pound the dough with a rolling pin several times to flatten the butter, then roll out three times as long as wide (18 inches). Fold the dough from one end to the center, and then fold the other end over that. It is important to keep a neat rectangle with neat edges and to work quickly so the butter doesn't get too soft. Wrap in aluminum foil and chill at least 30 minutes. Remove from refrigerator, roll to 18 inches long again, and fold as before. This is called a "turn." Give the dough at least five different turns with 30-minute intervals of chilling between turns. Always roll dough out lengthwise from short end to short end. Keep in refrigerator until ready to bake, or freeze for long keeping.

FRENCH FRUIT STRIP

>   ⅓ cup almond paste
>   5 egg whites

⅓ cup glazed fruit
¼ cup flour
¼ teaspoon salt
½ cup sugar
1 recipe Puff Paste (see page 174)

Smooth almond paste with about 1 tablespoon egg white. Mix the glazed fruit with the flour and add to the almond paste. Blend thoroughly. Beat remaining egg whites and the salt until frothy. Begin adding sugar 1 tablespoon at a time. Beat until all sugar is used and the meringue is stiff and glossy. Fold the almond paste and fruit mixture into the meringue. Roll out the Puff Paste ¼-inch thick on a lightly floured board. Cut a strip about 20 inches long and 6 inches wide. Put the strip on a baking sheet and spread with the meringue mixture, leaving ½-inch border of pastry all around. Moisten the border with water. Cut another strip the same size and place this strip over the filling. Press the edges together firmly. Brush the top with beaten egg and cut shallow diagonal lines on top. Bake in a hot (450°F.) oven for 15 minutes or until paste is puffed. Reduce heat to 350°F. and bake for 25 minutes, or until it is golden. Serve whole or cut along diagonal lines.

MERINGUE SHELLS

4 egg whites
½ teaspoon salt
1 teaspoon cream of tartar
1 cup sugar

Beat egg whites until frothy; sprinkle with salt and cream of tartar. Continue beating until stiff. Gradually beat in sugar, adding 2 tablespoons at a time; continue beating until stiff and peaked. With a pastry bag or spoon mound the meringue in bee-hive shapes on a greased baking sheet which has been covered with a lightly greased brown paper. Bake in a very slow (250°F.) oven 45 to 60 minutes, or until very delicately browned and dry. Remove from paper while still warm. Fill with ice cream or sherbet.

Makes about 10 meringue shells.

CHOCOLATE CAKE

½ cup butter
1¾ cups sugar
4 eggs, separated
2 cups sifted cake flour
½ teaspoon baking soda
1 teaspoon baking powder
¼ teaspoon salt
½ cup cocoa
1¼ cups milk
1 teaspoon vanilla
Whipped cream
Finely chopped almonds

Cream the butter until soft and smooth. Gradually add sugar, beating until the mixture is very light and fluffy. Beat in the egg yolks one at a time. Sift together the flour, baking soda, baking powder, salt, and cocoa. Add flour mixture alternately with the milk, beating until smooth after each addition. Add vanilla. Beat the egg whites until stiff but not dry; fold them into the batter. Pour into two 9- or 10-inch cake pans. Bake in a slow (325°F.)

oven for about 1 hour or until done. Fill and frost with a mixture of whipped cream and finely chopped almonds.

Makes two 9- or 10-inch layers.

HAZELNUT CAKE

    5 eggs
    1 cup sugar
    2 cups and 2 tablespoons sifted cake flour
    ¼ teaspoon salt
    ¼ cup coarsely ground hazelnuts

Beat the eggs with an electric mixer until they are light, fluffy, and lemon-colored. Add sugar slowly and continue beating. Blend sifted flour and salt and hazelnuts. Add flour mixture to eggs, beating constantly to blend thoroughly. Pour into an ungreased 10-inch tube pan. Bake in a moderate (350°F.) oven for 45 to 50 minutes or until done. Remove from oven and invert pan to cool.

Makes one 10-inch cake.

"SPONGE" CAKE

    1½ cups sugar
    ½ cup water
    7 egg whites
    1 teaspoon cream of tartar
    1 teaspoon vanilla
    Pinch of salt
    1 cup sifted cake flour

Boil 1 cup of sugar with the water until it forms a thread. Meanwhile, beat egg whites until they become foamy, then add cream of tartar. Continue beating until the egg whites are stiff, but not dry. Slowly add remaining ½ cup sugar and the vanilla. When syrup has cooled slightly, add—very slowly—to egg whites. When thoroughly blended, fold in flour and salt. Pour into an ungreased 10-inch tube pan. Bake in a moderate (375°F.) oven 30 to 35 minutes or until done. Invert pan for 1 hour or until cake is cool.

Makes one 10-inch cake.

PEACH BAVARIAN CREAM

    1 envelope plain gelatin
    ¼ cup cold water
    1½ cups scalded milk
    3 eggs, separated
    ⅓ cup sugar
    1 teaspoon vanilla, if desired
    1 cup drained, canned peach slices

Soften gelatin in cold water 5 minutes; add milk. Combine egg yolks and sugar, add gelatin mixture and cook over hot water 5 minutes, stirring constantly until sugar is dissolved. Cool and chill until slightly thickened. Add vanilla and fold in stiffly beaten egg whites. Place a few peach slices in parfait glasses or individual serving dishes and top with Bavarian Cream mixture. Chill before serving.

Serves 6.

RICE PUDDING

      1 cup rice
1½ quarts (6 cups) milk
      1 teaspoon salt
      ¼ teaspoon nutmeg
1½ teaspoons vanilla
      ¼ teaspoon cinnamon
      ¾ cup sugar
      1 egg, well beaten
      2 tablespoons melted butter

Add rice to milk seasoned with salt. Cook on top of range for 14 minutes. Season with nutmeg, vanilla, cinnamon, and sugar. Add egg and butter and mix well. Pour into a baking dish and brown lightly under the broiler. Allow to cool. Chill thoroughly before serving.

Serves 6.

Index